C000002985

DUDLEY &
NETHERTON
REMEMBERED

NED WILLIAMS

The
History
Press

THE BLACK COUNTRY SOCIETY

The Black Country Society is proud to be associated with **The History Press** of Stroud. In 1994 the society was invited to collaborate in what has proved to be a highly successful publishing partnership, namely the extension of the *Britain in Old Photographs* series into the Black Country. In this joint venture the Black Country Society has played an important role in establishing and developing a major contribution to the region's photographic archives by encouraging society members to compile books of photographs on the area or town in which they live.

The first book in the Black Country series was *Wednesbury in Old Photographs* by Ian Bott, launched by Lord Archer of Sandwell in November 1994. Since then over 70 Black Country titles have been published. The total number of photographs contained in these books is in excess of 13,000, suggesting that the whole collection is probably the largest regional photographic survey of its type in any part of the country to date.

The society, which now has over 2,500 members worldwide, organises a yearly programme of activities. There are six venues in the Black Country where evening meetings are held on a monthly basis from September to April. In the summer months, there are fortnightly guided evening walks in the Black Country and its green borderland, and there is also a full programme of excursions further afield by car. Details of all these activities are to be found on the society's website, **www.blackcountrysociety.co.uk**, and in *The Blackcountryman*, the quarterly magazine that is distributed to all members.

PO Box 71 · Kingswinford · West Midlands DY6 9YN

Title page: An electric tram climbs Castle Hill and makes its way past the Dudley Opera House in about 1910. Neither the trams nor the Opera House can be remembered by many current Dudley folk. Most of the images used in this book are related to the memories of those alive today – but they too will be consigned to history.

Opposite: Although in Worcestershire, these Netherton men at Noah Hingley's Ironworks were obviously proud of being able to produce a Staffordshire Knot in iron.

First published 2010

The History Press
The Mill, Brimscombe Port
Stroud, Gloucestershire, GL5 2QG
www.thehistorypress.co.uk

British Library Cataloguing in Publication Data.
A catalogue record for this book is available from the British Library.

ISBN 978 0 7524 5562 4

Typesetting and origination by The History Press
Printed in Great Britain

CONTENTS

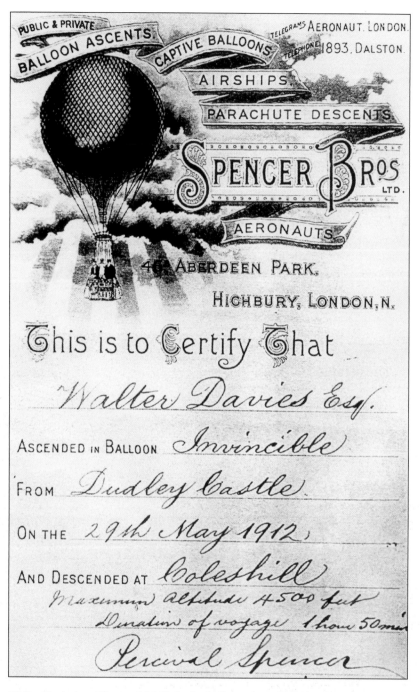

PUBLIC & PRIVATE
BALLOON ASCENTS
CAPTIVE BALLOONS
TELEGRAMS AERONAUT. LONDON.
TELEPHONE 1893, DALSTON.
AIRSHIPS
PARACHUTE DESCENTS
SPENCER BROS LTD.
AERONAUTS
46 ABERDEEN PARK,
HICHBURY, LONDON, N.

This is to Certify That

Walter Davies Esq.

ASCENDED IN BALLOON *Invincible*

FROM *Dudley Castle.*

ON THE *29th May 1912,*

AND DESCENDED AT *Coleshill*

Maximum altitude 4500 feet

Duration of voyage 1 hour 50 min

Percival Spencer

Walter Davies' certificate of 1912 for his balloon ascent from Dudley Castle. Wally was born in 1891 at Springs Mire and was educated at Holly Hall School. Having started work at The Earl's Ironworks at Brierley Hill in 1907, he later joined his brother-in-law, Sidney Bray, in Dudley's growing cinema business. Wally was more interested in being an inventor and specialised in aviation and hydro-gliding – all based in a workshop at 90 Aston Road! Dudley has many such stories.

INTRODUCTION

Welcome to another book about Dudley, the town that was my introduction to the West Midlands, and for many local people has been the capital of the Black Country. Today Dudley is looking for a new image and the flood of books about its past can only help us all piece together what we treasure about Dudley and what we hope might contribute to its future.

The medieval town that grew up in a 'saddle', within the ridge that divides the Black Country in two, was once small and compact. By the time Mr J. Treasure was drawing

Dudley Castle occupies the top right-hand corner of this aerial photograph of Dudley and enjoys a degree of permanence while everything else reflects restless change. The bus station in the centre of the picture has gone through many changes since it opened in 1951, replacing slums that had been a legacy of nineteenth-century Dudley. To the left is the Churchill Precinct – a monument to Dudley's self-confidence of the 1960s, and also visible is Cavendish House – a monument to how easy it is to make mistakes!

his map of the town in the early 1830s it was already beginning to expand in response to the industrialisation of the area. Already Dudley had 'suburbs' at Eve Hill and Kates Hill. Within a few decades it had industrial areas and large quantities of housing – most of which would have to be cleared in the twentieth century. Far from being healthy as a result of its altitude, Dudley was a very insalubrious place to live, although its Board of Health seemed to be working harder than its Town Commissioners to sort things out.

From 1865 onwards Dudley was granted Borough status and improvements began. In 1888 it became a County Borough and made various attempts to expand – the most notable being in the 1920s when Dudley absorbed the castle and the Earl of Dudley's Priory Estate – both of which had been in Staffordshire up until that time. The Dudley considered in this book is the Dudley that belonged within those frontiers – not the enlarged County Borough of 1966 or the even bigger Metropolitan Borough of 1974.

While thinking of borders it is interesting to note that Netherton was part of Dudley as defined by the 1865 boundary. This immediately brings up the question of whether Dudley is one town or whether its component parts almost have an independent existence of their own? I tried to recognise the particular claims of Netherton by producing two books devoted to just that township: *Netherton in Old Photographs* (Sutton Publishing, 2006) and *Netherton: People & Places* (The History Press, 2008). It seemed to prove that you could study Netherton without having to study Dudley, but that the reverse is not true. Later in 2008 I produced *Dudley Rediscovered* and tried to explain Dudley by breaking it down into its separate communities – examining them in the order in which they had become familiar to me as someone catapulted into the town in the autumn of 1962. The more one becomes acquainted with Eve Hill, Kates Hill, Holly Hall, etc., the more one appreciates their separateness – but that is true of many Black Country towns – they are simply federations of smaller units. In the case of Netherton it has an extra special kind of independence, and hence a chapter all of its own in this book.

This brings us to *Dudley & Netherton Remembered*; looking at the aspects of Dudley which are as much 'memories' as they are history – school days, a changing town centre, the community life of the town, the busy world of the churches and the growth of housing estates. In all these topics, the key word is change. The contents of a photograph are frozen forever, but the photograph quickly becomes proof that everything is changing. Chapters are devoted to topics omitted from the previous books – hence the space given to Dudley's schools, a topic central to so many peoples' memories.

1

DUDLEY'S TOWN CENTRE

D udley's town centre has always been compact and fairly well defined. It stretches from Castle Hill to Top Church and a little to each side of the main thoroughfare that widens at its central point to form a market place. On the site of Dudley's old Town Hall stands the magnificent fountain pictured below as our first image of the town centre.

What follows is an attempt to show that the town centre has gone through key periods of change; in Victorian times, between the two world wars and from the 1960s onwards. These periods of activity have all had their effect on Dudley's ability to claim it has a historic town centre that could now be cultivated as feature of the town and aid its regeneration.

The quality of Dudley's town centre cannot be divorced from the quality of the surrounding streets and that is a zone which has experienced very mixed fortunes, ranging from the nightmares of King Street, to gentle conservation areas and pleasant vistas.

The Fountain in Dudley's Market Place is an iconic image with which to begin our survey of the town. Dudley became a modern borough in 1865 and two years later the Countess of Dudley opened this fountain symbolising the progress the new authority was going to make. Clean drinking water and new street lighting were a few of the innovations to be enjoyed. The fountain was designed by James Forsyth who also designed the Earl's fountain at Witley Court. (*Tanfield's 'Views of Dudley'*)

This late nineteenth-century photograph of the Market Place looking towards the castle and St Edmund's Church emphasises just how wide the market patch really is. Menageries and travelling shows were able to set up in this space during the nineteenth century, but greater road space was needed after the arrival of the tramways. *(Tanfield's 'Views of Dudley')*

Looking along Castle Street in the 1900s. Our view is towards Castle Hill after the arrival of the tramtracks and it shows the cabmen's rest on the left of the picture, partly obscuring the Hen & Chickens Inn. The inn was later replaced with a building typical of the 1930s style. Steam trams had first invaded the centre of Dudley in 1884, but the route was electrified in 1899 and finally replaced with buses in 1930. *(Bytheway Collection)*

The electric tramway had to be built as single-track with passing loops to make its way through some of the narrow thoroughfares of Dudley. Certainly the High Street seems narrow here as it crosses Wolverhampton Street and Union Street. On the corner of the latter is the Old Bush – originally one of Dudley's coaching inns. On the corner of Wolverhampton Street (left) is an Edwardian building on a site now occupied by W.H. Smith. *(Bytheway Collection)*

This view of work progressing in Stone Street in the early 1950s provides a glimpse of the Criterion cinema. The cinema, in this form, had opened in 1923 and lasted until 1956. *(Bytheway Collection)*

Dudley's Market Place is still a good environment for public occasions. Here we see the Mercian Regiment parading and receiving the Freedom of the Borough on their return from the Middle East on 14 March 2008, as the mayor and official party look on from a platform in front of the fountain. *(NW)*

An atmospheric picture of the Market Place at night looking towards the fountain from between the market stalls. Although the fountain has benefited from at least one refurbishment, it generally seems a little 'unloved' today, despite the town's commitment to exploiting its heritage features. *(Roger Crombleholme)*

During the 1950s and early '60s a Christmas tree was placed in the Market Place as a present from Fort William to the people of Dudley. The link between Fort William and Dudley was forged by Bert Bissell, leader of the Vicar Street Men's Bible Class. His annual peace pilgrimages to the summit of Ben Nevis took many Dudley lads to the Scottish Highlands. *(Author's Collection)*

Dudley did not exercise its right to municipalise local passenger road transport and the trams were replaced with Midland Red buses. These eventually had to start and terminate at the bus station in Fisher Street – first opened in 1952. This area is now closed to all vehicular traffic at weekends, but getting buses in and out of Dudley is still a problem. *(Author's Collection)*

Dudley Council set about trying to improve and modernise the town centre in the late 1920s and into the 1930s. Improvements on one side of the town centre involved widening and straightening King Street, and connecting it more effectively with Trindle Road. On the Wolverhampton side of the town centre, streets were widened, new buildings were erected and the Civic Centre was started. In this photograph we look down New Street from the Market Place with new shops on the left built by the council in the early 1920s.

Looking up New Street towards the Market Place emphasises just how narrow New Street was at the time. *(Four photographs on this spread from the collection of Trevor Brook)*

A key building that had to be demolished to widen and improve New Street was the Baptist Chapel. This photograph also shows the side of the building in Tower Street. As a result of its demolition the Baptists gained a brand new chapel in Priory Road, opened on 24 September 1936. Transforming New Street and the way into Priory Road in the 1930s reflected the growth of that side of town, as well as improving the centre.

We look along Tower Street towards the castle from the same crossroads. Demolition here provided space for a new police station and fire station, and on the right the Court House was rebuilt as a modern 1930s public house.

The view along Tower Street from the Stone Street corner, with a view of the castle in the distance. Note the new façade of the Arcade on the right. This had been completed in 1925, replacing an old malthouse that had stood on the site. *(Trevor Brook)*

The old Town Hall on the corner of Priory Street and Priory Road was built by the Earl of Dudley in 1858 in anticipation of the demolition of a former town hall that existed in the Market Place (on the site where the fountain was built). This one was demolished in turn in 1933 to make way for the new Civic Centre and Council House. The foundation stone of the latter was laid in 1934 and the new building was opened on 2 December 1935 by the Duke of Kent. *(Stan Hill)*

This famous postcard view of the old police station in Priory Street shows us another part of Dudley that was scheduled for replacement in the 1930s. The new police station, however, did not open until 1941 and parts of this building survived. *(Stan Hill)*

Dudley's first fire station was provided in Priory Street in 1892 and was used as such until the service moved to Tower Street in 1941. It was later converted to Payne's shoe shop and also served as a café. In the background are the buildings of Stone Street, including the offices of Edwin Blocksidge, printer and publisher of the *Dudley Almanac*.

The 1930s saw a desire to modernise many of Dudley's services and infrastructure. This was nicely reflected in the building of the new Civic Centre in Priory Road. As one left the Market Place and turned into New Street, new council-built shops stood on one corner and a rebuilt version of the Hen & Chickens on the other. From 1941 onwards a new police station occupied the corner of Tower Street, opposite a 1930s rebuild of the Court House pub. As seen here in 2008, the police station has an excellent 'modern' entrance rather ruined by the addition of a ramp. Below, we see the new fire station in Tower Street, adjoining the police station, and also opened in 1941. *(NW and Paul Roberts)*

The Mayor of Dudley, Alderman William Wakeman, inspects the borough's latest ambulance in Tower Street in December 1955. Emergency services have now been relocated to Burton Road and this complex has been abandoned. *(Wakeman Collection)*

In the early 1980s the square in Stone Street became a temporary home for Dudley's market. As a trolleybus (and later a bus) terminus, it can be seen on page 18. In the background is the Library and Art Gallery of 1884, and, on the right, the Brooke Robinson Museum and the War Memorial Tower of the Town Hall, both opened on 16 October 1928. *(Author's Collection)*

Wolverhampton Corporation trolley bus no. 446 reaches the end of the 58 route as it swings from Priory Street into Stone Street in the mid-1960s. In the background is the fire station building (see page 15), the headquarters of the Midland Counties Mutual Benefit Society (founded in 1912) and the Crown. The car park on the left later became an archaeological site as seen on the opposite page. *(Roger Hodson)*

Three trolleybuses are fighting for space in this busy view of the Stone Street terminus – probably photographed on the last day of trolleybus operation: 3 March 1967. Note the façade of Dudley's 'Arcade' in the background, featuring Caswell's famous toyshop (formerly Woodworth's). On the left are the offices of Noel Thompson, auctioneers and surveyors in 22 Stone Street, next door to the premises once occupied by Edwin Blocksidge (see page 15). *(Roger Hodson)*

The square in the Stone Street area of Dudley has long played a key part in the life of the town centre. Surrounded by interesting and historic buildings, the square itself has seen a variety of uses: market place, turning circle and terminus for the Wolverhampton trolleybuses, car park and now a designated public space. In the eighteenth century the site was partly occupied by a flint glass works and in February 2003 the site was the centre of an archaeological dig, during the transition from car park to civic square. Here we see Cllr John Elliot and archaeologist Kate Brain examining the remains of glass cones that had been exposed. *(Express & Star)*

Bill Whittaker's Bedford OB stands in Stone Street in July 1992. In the background are the Brooke Robinson Museum, and the Town Hall's War Memorial Tower, opened by Stanley Baldwin in 1928. *(NW)*

Just as the 1930s had been a key decade in the development of Dudley, the 1960s also set out to modernise the town. The demolition of the old Hall Street and New Hall Street between the Market Place and the island between King Street and Trindle Road – both of which had been widened and improved in the 1930s – prepared the way for building a modern shopping precinct. This model shows the three-part structure of the developments very clearly: Birdcage Walk is on the right, and the two sections of the Churchill Precinct are on the left. *(From the precinct's opening brochure)*

A key feature of these developments was the separation of pedestrians from road traffic. Therefore, large car parks had to be provided on the flank of King Street in an area that had been cleared as a result of slum clearance in the Mambles and Flood Street areas. This 2008 view from Falcon House shows how the footbridge over King Street provided the essential link from the car parks to the precinct. By the end of the 1960s Dudley's postmark claimed the town's fame rested on shopping, the zoo, and car-parking! Cavendish House and Castle Hill feature on the horizon. *(NW)*

Birdcage Walk was the first part of the precinct to open, and this took place in April 1964. It took its name from the aviary provided by Dudley Zoo at the left-hand end of the promenade. At the right-hand end is the sculpted frieze by Bainbridge Copnall portraying local industry. The steps on the right led into a small car park, but this was later built upon to provide a home for C&A from 1981 to 1992, now a supermarket. This addition ruined the view from Birdcage Walk and turned it into the gloomy desolate concrete canyon that it has become. *(NW)*

The main thoroughfare of the precinct, seen here, followed the line of Hall Street, which it had replaced. It was finished in 1967, two years before the final stage was completed for a grand opening on 8 September 1969. The 1960s also saw many premises in the Market Place replaced with modern buildings. *(NW)*

Once the Churchill Precinct was completed, the Town Clerk, Percy Wadsworth, looked around for someone to be the centre's manager and take responsibility for its security. He appointed Mick Coyle, issued him with a uniform and installed him in a bungalow on the roof car park of the centre, where we see him above.

Mick Coyle was greatly assisted in his work once issued with a guard dog called Rex, and together they maintained order in the precinct. His duties ranged from feeding the parrots in the aviary in Birdcage Walk to crowd-control during bread strikes (see next page).

Mick Coyle was born in Fountain Street in 1925 only to be moved to the Wren's Nest Estate in 1939 – from which he joined the Navy. He came to the centre from a job as caretaker at Bishop Milner School. *(Mick Coyle)*

During a 1970s bread strike, Mick Coyle had to erect barricades in the Churchill Precinct to control the queues outside Tommy Tucker's Bakery. He provided tea and coffee for people in the queue and ensured access to the other shops. His work made him a well-known figure in Dudley – equally well known as a charity fundraiser and supporter of many local causes. *(Mick Coyle Collection)*

The Trident Centre was opened on 11 September 1973 by Cllr C.E. Clarke – four years after the first property had been purchased to prepare the site. It stretched from this High Street entrance round to Wolverhampton Street and was designed by Alan Young & Partners and Messrs Webb & Gray – all local architects. It was built by Bovis Construction. Like the Churchill Precinct it was promoted as a development that would enhance the town centre and ensure that Dudley had a great future as a retail centre. Sainsbury's were the major tenant and car parking was integrated into the centre's design. *(Author's Collection)*

The Churchill Precinct and the Trident Centre were both symbols of Dudley's pride in being a retail centre, but after the opening of the Merry Hill Shopping Complex a few miles away, the town's fortunes as a retail centre have seemed to decline. Shops like Marks & Spencer and British Home Stores withdrew their presence, and long-established local family businesses disappeared from the scene. Beatties maintained their department store in the Churchill Precinct and it seemed that the flag of Woolworths would fly forever in the Market Place. Woolworths had 1,000 stores in Britain by 1958, but in December 2008 the firm went into administration. Dudley's branch of 'Woolies' closed on 27 December 2008 and is seen here boarded up immediately afterwards. *(NW)*

Beatties store finally closed on 23 January 2010, a week earlier than expected, and the staff, led by Manager Karen Morris, put on a brave face and posed for a final farewell photograph. The clearance sale kept the shop busy until the end but it was a sad day for Dudley's survival as a retail centre. While House of Fraser were busy announcing the store's closure, the regeneration officers were stating their aim of attracting a new major retailer to the centre of Dudley. *(Express & Star)*

2

DUDLEY ZOO

The Dudley Zoological Society was founded in 1935 by Alfred Marsh and the Earl of Dudley, and the zoo was opened on 6 May 1937. The animals started arriving in the preceding month, some coming from Oxford Zoo. (The very first arrivals were three peacocks presented by the Duke of Sutherland.) The most exciting animals to arrive were two young Indian elephants, Maharenee and Yuvarajah, who travelled to Dudley by rail.

It was not only the animals that made Dudley Zoo interesting – the project was also a bold architectural adventure in which Berthold Lubetkin's 'Tecton' group of designers produced a number of buildings in modern style clustered around the steep sides of the hill and providing an imposing entrance. The team had already produced buildings at London Zoo and at Whipsnade but the hill-top setting of Dudley Zoo was seen as an ideal location for such innovative designs. Today twelve of these structures are listed and are of great interest to architectural students, but their qualities are not exploited in the promotion of the zoo. The entrance, although preserved, is not really used as an entrance, and the pavilions are rather lost among over sixty later buildings which have no particular architectural style or interest. The best survivors include the Bear Ravine, the Polar Bear Pit, and the Bird House, but the famous Penguin Pool has been demolished.

The Lubetkin entrance to Dudley Zoo on Castle Hill is truly a landmark feature of Dudley and is seen here in the summer of 2007 when the zoo was celebrating its 70th Anniversary. Note the out-of-use chairlift in the background. *(NW)*

The ponies presented at Dudley Zoo were trained by the Edgbaston Riding School in Birmingham and are seen here on the Hagley Road advertising the zoo and the pony rides. In the centre of the picture is Edith Stewart (née Parker) from Holly Hall who was 'mad about animals' and enjoyed working with the ponies before the Second World War. *(Edith Stewart via Tony Stewart)*

Although not completed, the zoo was opened on 6 May 1937, just ahead of Whitsun and the Coronation of George VI on 19 May, both of which were major public holidays. This picture of the Bear Pit was taken on Coronation Day. Although it was anticipated that the zoo would have an official opening later in 1937, the events of 6 May felt like a proper opening, with speeches galore in the Zoological Club. *(R. Hood)*

One of the most important things about Dudley Zoo is its location on the slopes of Castle Hill. This 1959 photograph manages to combine the zoo elements of the site and the existence, in the midst of all this, of the castle. *(Bill Bawden)*

The complete story of all the animals that have arrived at and departed from Dudley Zoo has yet to be told. In 1958 three baby tigers arrived from Copenhagen Zoo and one of them is seen here in the isolation unit with Barry Foley. Perhaps the most famous arrival at Dudley Zoo was Cuddles (a Killer Whale), who arrived in the early 1970s from Don Robinson's Flamingo Land. Cuddles was housed in a dolphin pool which many thought was inadequate, but died in April 1974 before his pool could be improved. *(Barry Foley)*

This picture of Meena the elephant giving children a ride was used in zoo publicity material, but it showed something slightly unusual in that the number of children allowed to ride on each side of the seat on the elephant's back was strictly limited to four. In this instance three-year-old Ann Griffiths was permitted to join her brother David for the ride.

Dudley Zoo's miniature railway was installed just before the Second World War by a syndicate led by Trevor Guest, a director of a Stourbridge building firm. He built several of the locomotives that worked on the line. It began as a 10¼in gauge railway but was re-laid in 1946 to a gauge of 15in to cope with greater traffic. Trains were usually propelled out of the station and hauled back along the side of Castle Hill – there was no station at the 'other end'. It went through several changes of management and modifications, and closed altogether in September 1992. This pre-war postcard showed Maharanee inspecting one of the Guest-built locomotives. *(Fay Davis)*

Dudley Zoo Railway photographed on 4 April 1943 when laid to the original gauge of 10¼in. The GWR 'Saint'-styled 4–6–0 locomotive no. 3, built by Twinings Models Ltd., is about to enter the station beneath the original signal gantry. (*L.W. Perkins/Alan Wycherley Collection*)

Dudley Zoo Railway seen in September 1951 with the railway now laid with 15in gauge track. The LMS Class 'V'-styled engine, named *Prince Charles* built in 1946 by Trevor Guest is seen on the train. This locomotive also saw use on the Fairbourne Railway in Wales. Note the railcar in the shed. (*L.W. Perkins/Alan Wycherley Collection*)

The chairlift was a popular feature of Dudley Zoo and was opened on 22 August 1958. Ten-year-old John Price is seen here trying it out on the first day of operation. For over forty years it carried passengers on a 125ft journey up and down Castle Hill, but it was closed in 2000 because of concerns regarding its safety. There had not been any accidents on the lift, although people were stranded on it during a power cut in May 1997. Currently, plans to improve the zoo include the restoration of the chairlift in a modified form. (*Express & Star*)

The zoo's animals often left the zoo to take part in activities in and around Dudley in what would now be called 'photo opportunities'. Here we see the elephants joining the guests at the wedding of Arthur and Freda Parkes in about 1957, at St Francis's Church in the Priory Estate. Arthur ran a radio & TV shop in Wolverhampton Street but also looked after the sound system in the Queen Mary Ballroom in the zoo. (*Bytheway Collection*)

3

TOWN LIFE

Looking at the pages of the *Dudley Herald* in the archives, it is impossible to imagine that Dudley was anything but a very lively place – positively buzzing with civic, social and communal activities at every level from street and neighbourhood to the entire town. The churches, schools, sporting activities, pubs, college rag week, etc., all contributed to this in a way that has disappeared in recent decades.

There were bold attempts to mobilise the whole of Dudley in celebrating events like the carnivals of 1929 and 1930, and the pageant of 1951, and of course there were hundreds of much more local events in Woodside, Netherton, Kates Hill, Eve Hill, and the new estates. There were also big occasions when the town hosted royalty, or celebrated coronations or the ends of wars.

The social character of a town like Dudley can best be understood in terms of the lives of its citizens – some well-known, some eventually forgotten. This chapter takes us through Dudley's past via the lives of mayors, figures from the civic, social, cultural and sporting life of the borough, and key events like carnivals and festivals. This picture, taken on 14 July 1934, is a little 'Who's Who' of Dudley past. Alderman Ballard is seen on the left, just five months before his death. The lady is Dorothy Round (Dudley's famous tennis champion), greeted by the Mayor of Dudley, Alderman Williams, and Dudley Joel, the town's MP. Each of these people had a story to tell – in which Dudley played a major part. They stand at the County Cricket Ground . . . and that's another story!

The 1929 Dudley Carnival Committee, chaired by Alderman Ballard. He and his wife, the Mayoress of Dudley, sit either side of Joyce Raybould, the carnival queen. In the back row, left to right, are: Miss M. Lane, Mr Jupp the carnival director, Miss Clarke and Miss Harley, Mr H. Raybould the treasurer, and Miss Simmons. John Molyneux, the deputy chairman of the committee is missing, as is Albert Martin the 'King of Mirth'. *(R. Hood Collection)*

THE 1929 CARNIVAL

F.J. Ballard, the Mayor of Dudley, and Alderman John Molyneux, his 'deputy', put their heart and soul into establishing the first Dudley Carnival, and with their carnival director, Mr I.J. Jupp, they were rewarded with great success – both in terms of raising money for local charities and in creating an event that brought Dudley folk together in a sense of community. The Dudley Guest Hospital was trying to raise £50,000 at the time, and the carnival raised about a tenth of this sum.

The carnival was held in the third week of September (15–21) and the week was packed with events both in the town centre and in Dudley's 'suburbs'. (Netherton had already held its own very successful carnival in the previous month – as if determined to lead the way in these matters.) The main events began in the Castle Grounds on the Monday night when the town was 'surrendered' to thirty-seven pirates and Joyce Raybould, the Carnival Queen, was crowned. At the other end of the week the appearance of Lady Godiva (Miss Lucielle Smith) rather stole the show!

Pat Collins, the Black Country showman, was asked to put on his fair on the Trindle Road ground, and despite the fact that it was at his busiest time of the year, he presented a memorable fair at which the Wall of Death made its local debut. The week featured processions, dances and sporting events, all of which were well supported – possibly Dudley's finest hour in terms of presenting itself as a single community enjoying itself.

Alderman Molyneux (centre of back row) and his Dudley Carnival group of 1930. Also seen here are the 'King of Mirth' (Albert Martin) and the carnival queen (Winnie Molyneux – also the Mayoress!), and attendants. *(R. Hood Collection)*

THE 1930 CARNIVAL

After the great success of Dudley's first twentieth-century carnival in 1929 there were high hopes that the event could be repeated, and that it would be a confirmation of Dudley's civic pride and sense of community. For some reason, and no two people agreed why, success was not repeated financially. Gross income dropped from £5,000 to £1,500 and local charities received only £800 after expenses had been met.

In August 2000 there was an attempt to revive the idea of a Dudley Carnival but it was met with a poor response. Here we see the floats moving off from Blowers Green Road for a journey to Grange Park. *(NW)*

After the great Dudley Carnivals of 1929 and 1930, the town does not seem to have staged a major civic festival until 1951 when the Festival of Britain revived enthusiasm for the communal celebration of national and local identity. The town council controversially voted in favour of the sum of £4,000 towards the staging of a grand local pageant to be presented in Dudley Castle. Gwen Lally was appointed to direct the pageant and Mr Helliwell, the Borough Librarian, became 'Pageant Master' – hundreds of Dudley people became involved. The show presented nine episodes in Dudley's history starting with Queen Elizabeth I's visit of 1575, seen above. Below is a shot of the seating for 2,500 people that was provided, and even atrocious weather did not put off the audience!

June Sidaway (née Wakeman), photographed at the end of the last performance of the Pageant – just before going to the party! June had won a drama prize for her part in *Twelfth Night* while at the Gilbert Claughton Grammar School, and was remembered when it came to answering an advert in the *Dudley Herald* for roles in the Pageant, and auditioning for a part. June played Lady Catherine of Dudley and while doing so met her future husband, Vic Sidaway – then a student at Dudley Teacher Training College – who was playing the part of a herald. The Pageant brought a lot of Dudley people together and played a large part in their lives. *(June Sidaway)*

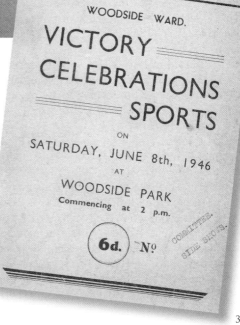

Souvenir Programme

WOODSIDE WARD.

VICTORY CELEBRATIONS SPORTS

ON

SATURDAY, JUNE 8th, 1946

AT

WOODSIDE PARK

Commencing at 2 p.m.

6d. N̲o̲

COMMITTEE.
SIDE SHOWS.

Although the Pageant of 1951 brought together people from all parts of the borough in an exercise of identifying with the town's past, it has to be remembered that many of the 'districts' of Dudley often enjoyed putting on much more local events that are generally less well recorded photographically. For example, only this programme seems to survive to remind us of the Woodside Victory Celebrations of June 1946. It was organised by Cllrs Clemson and Pearson plus J.H. Greenaway and W.S. Bloore. As well as sporting activities there was a carnival, bowls tournament, cycle races, dances, and a band concert featuring the Quarry Bank Silver Band. Prizes consisted of National Savings Certificates. *(Val Worwood)*

John Harry Molyneux was born in March 1882 in Pitfield Street – a narrow street running from Steppingstone Street to Greystone Street at the upper end of 'The Old Dock'. He was elected to the council in 1919, and is seen here in the robes and regalia of the Mayor of Dudley In a life devoted to the town, he found himself involved in many areas of Dudley's life – the Co-op, the football club, the council and much more. Today he has a street named after him in Netherton, but as an individual he is probably forgotten. In resurrecting his memory here we have to remember that there have been many such individuals in Dudley's history, but he provides us with an excellent example of such people's lives.

JOHN HARRY MOLYNEUX

John Harry Molyneux deserves to be remembered in Dudley for several reasons. Firstly he was the town's longest-serving member of the council. He was first elected to the council, to represent St John's ward, in 1919 and only retired from public life in April 1966 when local government was reorganised. He was four times mayor: in 1929, 1930, 1949, and briefly in 1933 after the death of H.J. Golding (see *Netherton: People & Places*, p. 67). He was made an alderman in 1930 and served as a justice of the peace from 1929 to 1957. For almost the entire time that he was on the council, he served on the Housing Committee – he was a passionate supporter of municipal housing and lived for years in such a house – at 28 Buns Lane. He was responsible for torching the notorious temporary 'hutments' provided for munitions workers during the First World War, and for making sure that modern council houses replaced them.

He had been a founder member of Dudley Labour Party and was the town's first Labour councillor, then mayor and alderman, but his life was more than just politics. He was a keen sportsman and had played for Dudley Town and Stafford Rangers. He led Dudley Town when they left their original home on the old football pitch at Shavers End and took up residence at the Birmingham Road ground. He also supported the Dudley Co-operative Society and was elected to its Board of Management in 1924, and then became the society's treasurer – a post he held until 1951 when he became the society's president. His name pops up in many areas of local life.

Molyneux was born in Pitfield Street in March 1882, and started work as a pattern-maker when he was thirteen. His memories of that street, with its lack of running water and dimly oil-lit houses, possibly inspired his interest in housing improvements. While still at school he worked evenings and Saturdays at a barber's and newsagency in Hall Street – often working until late at night.

Sir John Molyneux outside his home at 28 Buns Lane. It is perhaps fitting that someone who grew up in the poor conditions of Dudley's 'old housing' and who then devoted much energy to the improvement of the town, should have lived out his life in a council house built in the first wave of providing better homes for local people as a public venture.

The quest for employment took him to Stafford and Wolverhampton, but by the time of the 1901 Census he was to be found back in Kates Hill, Dudley, at 21 Hill Street. He became a trade unionist and played an active part in the United Pattern-Makers' Association, which was probably his introduction to the Labour Movement. He was in the union for fifty-six years and served ten years as Midland District President. Interestingly he formed his own pattern-making business in 1933 and kept that going until 1956.

John Molyneux was first elected to the council on 1 November 1919: he and Barney Norton from Netherton being the first Labour Party members to succeed in this endeavour. Apathy seemed to surround the election, despite the fact that women had just won the vote. Only half the electorate of St John's ward bothered to vote and John received 875 votes compared to his opponent's 755. The local press made little comment on his success. More attention was paid to Charlie Sitch's Labour victory in the earlier General Election when he won the Kingswinford seat. Sitch, Norton and John Molyneux were all strong trade unionists.

He first became Mayor of Dudley in September 1929, just after the town's first successful carnival, in which he had played a part. While mayor he presided over the second carnival of 1930, but without the same success. His wife had died in 1928 and therefore he gave the job of mayoress to his daughter Winifred who, at the time, was a twenty-one-year-old teacher at the Wolverhampton Street School.

His huge contribution to Dudley's civic life earned him many honours. He was given the OBE in 1956 and was then granted the Freedom of the Borough in 1959. The Freedom of the Borough was awarded at a joint ceremony held for him and Cyril Lord who had enjoyed a career that included being a local councillor, the town's MP, and the Executive Director of Noah Hingley's of Netherton. The only thing both men had in common was that they had started work as pattern-makers!

He was knighted on 1 March 1966, and later Dudley Council gave him a jewelled badge which he could wear to underline that he was now Sir John Molyneux – the sixth Dudley citizen to have that honour until that time. He may well have wanted to pursue his political interest further, because in 1945 he was shortlisted as a possible prospective parliamentary candidate for Dudley. In the end his friend George Wigg was selected and won the seat in the 1945 election. He also enjoyed other honours such as the Freedom of the Co-operative Society, which was granted in the autumn of 1959.

Despite the length of his political career, his terms of mayoral office and his honours, he seems to have remained fairly modest and certainly very straightforward in his dealings with others, whatever their political persuasion. He had a reputation for having his 'feet on the ground' and an ability to talk 'common sense'.

Sir John Molyneux died on 3 February 1968, aged 85. Until that time he still resided at 28 Buns Lane – a house he shared with his daughter, Mrs Winifred Southan, who in later years taught at Kates Hill Junior School. His other daughter, Vera, had married a Mr Watson, but neither daughter appears to have had children.

A funeral service was held at Top Church and it is interesting to see the immense variety of organisations represented there. The Mayor of Dudley, Cllr Caleb Homer, was there as we would expect, as well as many other councillors and council staff. George Wigg was present as well as John Gilbert, the prospective Labour MP for Dudley. Representatives of the Labour Movement, including the Trades Council, were joined by folks from four local Co-operative Societies, the Worcestershire Regiment, the Dudley Cricket Club and the Vicar Street Young Men's Bible Class. He was cremated at Gornal Crematorium.

Some years later, in 1983, his daughter Vera presented a special medical bath to the Woodlands Old People's Home in memory of her father and her sister.

With or without his robes, the mayor has to wear his chain and its pendant at all public occasions. Here we see Alderman James Smellie performing his mayoral duties on 4 October 1933 as he attends the laying of the foundation stone of the town's technical college (see page 86) with Mr Fisher, a former Minister of Education.

Alderman Francis James Ballard was born in 1876 and became another champion of Netherton when first elected to the council in 1912. However, as time went on, he became a great promoter of the whole of Dudley's well-being – not just the ward he represented. He chaired committees on Public Health and Public Works and was very active in planning Dudley's inter-war renaissance, including the Priory Estate (see page 88) and the new municipal buildings. He was mayor from 1927 to 1928 and played his part in the first Dudley Carnival. He owned an engineering firm in Tividale but was also interested in the local cinema business. He died on 23 December 1934 at Stourton.

Below, right: The pendant worn on the mayor's chain of office carries an image similar to the central portion of the town's crest adopted in 1866. It featured the keep of Dudley Castle, a miner's lamp, a limestone fossil, an anchor and the salamander. On leaving office the mayor is given the badge illustrated below.

As the town's 'First Citizen', a mayor's year of office often provides a visual scrapbook of the life and times of the town – if the mayor kept a photo album and if it has survived! In the case of William Wakeman (1900–88) a number of his photographs have survived in the family archives. He spent his entire working life on the local railway system (1915–62) and in 1955 became the first Mayor of Dudley to come from Netherton since the death of Mayor Henry Golding (who died while in office in 1933). He is seen here on 11 May 1956 at a meeting of the Industrial Life Assurance Officers' Association, along with the Mayor of Stourbridge on the left, and Cllr Stan Hill, proudly wearing his chain of office as Chairman of Brierley Hill Urban District Council. Ten years later Dudley would swallow up Brierley Hill and the next generation of mayors would have to come from a wider area.

William Wakeman's wife Rose became his mayoress, and was elected to the council as an independent during her year of office. Rose was also a magistrate from 1956 to 1970 and sat on the board of governors of local schools. Here we see Rose Wakeman, as mayoress, touring a schools exhibition at Dudley Town Hall on 13 March 1956. Local schoolgirls look on as she inspects examples of the craft work on display. *(Wakeman Collection)*

Another aspect of the mayor's role is to welcome overseas visitors to the Mayor's Parlour, on behalf of the town. Dudley built up all sorts of overseas connections over the years, although never adopted a twin-town. Here we see Mayor Wakeman, and Rose Wakeman, greeting some Norwegian Folk Dancers in 1955. *(Wakeman Collection)*

William and Rose Wakeman also met members of many of the local organisations which added to the life of the town. Here they pose with members of Dudley Golf Club at a dance at the Queen Mary Ballroom on 25 November 1955. The club has an interesting history, starting out with a nine-hole course on 'The Old Park' before moving to Oakham. *(Wakeman Collection)*

By the 1960s it was recognised that promoting a sense of community could be facilitated by providing a centre in which to meet. When Dudley CBC took over Brierley Hill UDC in 1966, they found it was a policy at which their neighbours had been very good. One approach was to attach a centre to a school – as provided here in Woodside.

A much-refurbished Woodside Community Centre was reopened on 3 September 2009 by the Mayor, Cllr Pat Martin, seen here with John Pestana, the centre's chairman and children from the centre's youth club. *(NW)*

When the Prince of Wales visited Dudley on 13 June 1923, his itinerary had to balance the claims of Woodside and Netherton to be as important as the centre of town. He therefore entered the borough by road at Netherton and first paid a visit to Noah Hingley's Ironworks. He then travelled on to the Drill Hall in Trinity Road before reaching the Town Hall at 11 o'clock in the morning. He also had to visit Messrs Harper & Bean's factory and the Guest Hospital, before leaving for lightning visits to Tipton and Wolverhampton. This left the mayor and all his guests with nothing to do but have lunch at the Dudley Arms Hotel before popping over to Woodside in the afternoon to unveil this war memorial. At first reading it almost suggests the Prince of Wales had managed to get to Woodside, but that was not the case! *(NW)*

Edward, The Prince of Wales, alights from his car at 1 o'clock outside Dudley Town Hall to be greeted by the Mayor of Dudley, Cllr Thomas William Tanfield. His visit was part of a programme in which he was to familiarise himself with the plight of the unemployed and veterans of the First World War. *(R. Hood Collection)*

Dudley, like everywhere else, has been visited by royalty on several occasions, starting with the visit on 13 June 1923 mentioned on the previous page. Two years later the Duke and Duchess of York arrived at Dudley station to help a fund-raising campaign for the Guest Hospital. We see them welcomed by the official party above – and note the reminder that Dudley was a joint GWR and LMS station! Princess Mary opened the extensions to the hospital in 1930, and in 1934 the Duke of Kent opened the new Council House. Queen Elizabeth II came on 23 June 1957 – seen below with the Mayor of Dudley, Cllr Sammy Danks – and again on 27 July 1977, her Silver Jubilee year.

For many people the life of a town is experienced in the routines of going to work or going shopping. The vitality of the town's shopping areas is a good indicator of the town's health, yet there is no aspect of a town that is more subject to change. Many Dudley folk will recall High Street names like F.W. Cook, or Bunce's and Bunney's seen here on the right-hand side of the street in about 1920. *(Ken Rock)*

The history of Dudley's shops progresses from many locally owned family businesses through the arrival of the 'multiples' to the emergence of the national chains and supermarkets. Here we see an advert for James Evans' grocery and provision store at 111 and 112 Hall Street in about 1905. By the First World War this shop had been taken over and absorbed into the George Mason empire – a form in which it survived until the 1960s programme of replacing Hall Street with a modern precinct. Hanging meat from the front of the shop is no longer a feature of such shops. George Mason was born in Shropshire and opened the first shop in his own name in 1909 in Lozells Road, Birmingham. When he died in Wolverhampton in 1934 he owned 500 shops, two of which were in Dudley, plus one in Netherton.

At one time both Dudley town centre and the outlying districts were host to many small family-run businesses. In the town centre these shops have given way to branches of national chains, and in the areas like Wolverhampton Street and Hall Street, the family businesses have gone through a long decline, even if managed by several generations of the same family. Here at 150 Wolverhampton Street was Bytheway's newsagency, with Elizabeth Bytheway in the doorway in the 1930s. Her son, Donald, ran the shop until 1983. At some stage the left-hand side of the premises returned to residential use but the right-hand side is still in use a shop. Not far away, at 167 Wolverhampton Street, was another newsagency run by the Burgin family through five generations, now claiming to be the oldest newsagency run by one family in the Midlands.

Frank Dyce's ice cream van stands by the wall of Jesson's School, opposite his shop in Wolverhampton Street in the 1920s. Jack made his ice cream in small premises at the far end of Salop Street. Note the traction pole on the left. *(Frank Dyce)*

Wolverhampton Street is now but a shadow of its former self (an attempt to do justice to its better days was presented in *Dudley Rediscovered* on p. 21–42). Here is Joseph Badley's ironmongery at 37 Wolverhampton Street, seen in the 1950s. Mrs Annie Brown, Joseph's sister, often helped out in the shop and is seen in the doorway. *(Bill Morgan)*

Jack Dyce outside his shop on Wolverhampton Street in the 1920s where he sold sweets, some groceries and his home-made ice cream. He ceased trading in about 1938 and the shop was unused until taken over by the Harris family who ran a greengrocery, but it later became known as a splendid fish and chip shop. Although this end of Wolverhampton Street (Eve Hill) is now much changed, a fish and chip shop still operates on the site. *(Frank Dyce)*

In 1948 the Post Office telegraph boys in Dudley were given 250cc BSA motorcycles to replace their former red push-bikes to aid faster delivery of telegrams. Left to right: Ron Guest, Ronnie Evans, Wilf Poultney (in charge of telegram delivery), Harry Shaw and Norman Taylor. Ron Guest gave forty-six years' service to the Post Office – eventually retiring as an area delivery manager, but he was beaten by his father who had managed forty-seven years' service! The picture is taken in the yard behind the main post office on the corner of Priory Street and Wolverhampton Street – alas no longer serving the postal needs of the community. *(Ron Guest)*

Play for your local pub team and see the world! In the 1980s the football team from the Malt Shovel in Tower Street went to Tours in France to play in an international tournament sponsored by Calberson, a haulage company. *(Paul Garner)*

ne Dudley Wednesday Football Club – so called because they all worked in shops and had to play football
1 early closing day! They played on the Shavers End Ground also used by Dudley Town Football Club before
1e First World War. Top right in back row is Harold Wythes. *(John Wythes)*

Voodside Wanderers were a famous Dudley football team. They played on Woodside Park in the Halesowen
outh League and were managed by Major Wesson who kept the Crown public house in Woodside. Back
ow, left to right: Tommy Bate and Hughie Johnson (committee members), Colin Beasley, Major Wesson,
enny Bailey, Freddy Brookes, Leslie Ward, Richard Greenaway (goalkeeper), Tommy Hawthorn, John
/ythes, Leslie Wood, Joe Edwards, ? Totney, Joey Wood. Front row: Micky Edwards, Billy Welsh, Sidney
obinson, Maurice Sherwood, Ray Wright, and Graham Mason. *(John Wythes)*

The photographs on this page are reproduced here to portray Dudley as a place of work. Above we see th[e] staff of the goods department of the LMS (London, Midland & Scottish Railway) outside the goods depot a[t] Dudley station. The group includes the agent himself, plus his clerical staff and the drivers, and one drive[r] has decided to include his horse! *(Doreen Gripton)*

Here we meet the employees of the West Midlands Gas Board based at Dudley.

4

DUDLEY'S
SCHOOLS

D udley's first schools were provided by charities during the eighteenth century, plus, of course, the Grammar School with a history going back to 1562. In the nineteenth century the Church of England, the Non-conformists and later the Roman Catholics also decided it was their duty to provide education, assisted by money from the state. The state itself became a player following the 1870 Education Act and the establishment of local school boards who set out to provide a more secular approach to the provision of schools. By the time the Dudley School Board was created there were five church schools operating in Dudley: St James's at Eve Hill (1842), St Edmund's on Castle Hill (1847), St John's on Kates Hill (1848) and St Thomas's (1848). There was also an inter-denominational school in Stafford Street dating from 1834. The Roman Catholics also added St Joseph's in the nineteenth century.

The Dudley School Board built eight new schools between 1870 and 1903 when it was dissolved and its powers absorbed by Dudley Borough Council. The board schools had provided 'elementary' education for five- to twelve-year-olds, so provision for extended education had to come from elsewhere for those willing or able to pay. Thus Dudley Proprietary School for Girls was opened in 1881, becoming a Municipal High School in 1904 and then becoming the Girls' High School in 1910.

By 1905 Dudley Council's schools were: Wolverhampton Street (boys, girls and infants), Park (boys, girls and infants), Harts Hill (mixed and infants), Kates Hill (boys,

he foundation stone
f the Upper Standard
chool, Blowers Green
oad, was laid on 20 May
903 by George Dunn,
hairman of the School
oard. Ten days later
he first meeting was
eld of Dudley Council's
ducation Department
nd the School Board
eased to exist. George
unn was its first
hairman. *(NW)*

girls and infants), Holly Hall (mixed and infants), Tetnall Street (infants only), plus the church school mentioned above, a Municipal Art School (St James's Road) and a School of Science and Commerce in Stafford Street. The Upper Standard School in Blowers Green Road was planned by the board, but was opened by Dudley's Education Committee. There were also four ex-board schools in Netherton, Northfield Road, the Brewery Street School, the 'Iron Schools' in Halesowen Road and an infant school in Dudley Wood, plus the Netherton C of E school on the corner of Church Road.

One or two noteworthy schools were built between the wars – such as the primary school at Dudley Wood which was much promoted as being in the new 'fresh air' style, and a post-war response to the 1944 Education Act was led by the provision of Hillcrest School, designed to be a prototype on which new secondary modern schools could be modelled.

Dudley Proprietary School for Girls opened on 28 April 1881 in premises on the corner of Wolverhampton Street and Trinity Road, starting with only twenty-four girls aged between seven and fourteen. Such was its success that the school moved into this grand English Gothic building in St James's Road, next door to the library and art gallery. This was extended in the mid-1890s. In 1904 it was acquired by Dudley and operated until 1910 as the Dudley Municipal High School. On 16 September the foundation stones were laid for a new, bigger building in Priory Road. This opened on 8 December 1910 as the Girls' High School in the form seen below. *(Joyce Garner)*

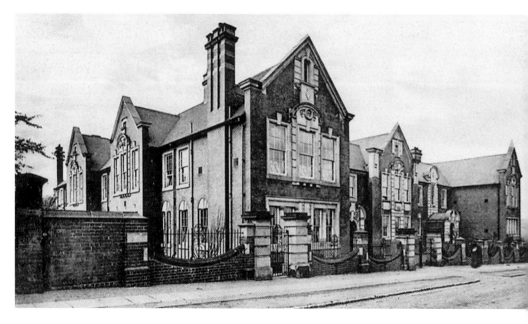

udley Girls' High School was a joint venture by Dudley County Borough and Staffordshire County Council.
he school took off in 1914 when Miss Frood became headmistress. She stayed until 1941. Although her
assion was the arts, the school provided a full range of subjects including science. Here is the science lab
1927.

he Girls' High School staff of 1959/60. At this time Miss Ambrose was the school's headmistress
1941–64), and she can be seen in the centre of the picture.

Dudley Girls' High School pupils. Here we see Mandy Beresford, Sandra Clarke, Jane Eley, Sheila Cox, Jill Dudley, Vanessa Andrews, Judith Billingham, Dianne Castree, Glynis Edwards, Amanda Fellows, Jane Dunn, Gudrun Elwell, Christine Ford, Cheryl Broome, Pat Conway and others in about 1973. *(Judith Round Collection)*

A painting by Gwen Jennings of Dudley Girls' High School was presented to Dudley Libraries in 2003 and is displayed on the main straicase in Dudley Central Library. In the autumn of 1999, a small group of former staff and pupils decided to write up the history of the school and publish their findings in a book. The book was launched in October 2002 and therefore the school has put a better record of its history in the public domain than most others. *(School Archives)*

At Dudley Girls' High School Miss Cooper and the Fifth Form are seen here in about 1950, proudly wearing their summer 'uniforms'. At the time clothes rationing meant that only the winter uniform was strictly a uniform. Back row, left to right: Norma Fellows, June Ellis, Barbara Fisher, Judith Edwards, Doreen Forrest, Pat Cartwright, Pauline Forrest, Doris Beardsmore, Betty Butler, Christine Coakley, Judith Carter, Geraldine Brookes. Middle row: Brenda Davies, Pat Saunders, Joyce Geddes, Janet Danks, Sylvia Crisp, Kay Grant, Maureen Baxter, Norma Baker, Shelagh Bennett, Pat Brownhill, Janice Watson. Front row: Jean Fellows, Sheila Dudley, Irene Armour, Freda Earp, Miss Cooper, Megan Bullock, Edna Foster, Joyce Bedford, Dorothy Gill. *(Joyce Garner née Bedford)*

The Dudley Girls' High School netball team, including Shirley Courtney, Margaret Greenway, Joyce Bedford, Dorothy Skidmore, Sheila White and Heather Southall, seen here in about 1950. *(Joyce Garner née Bedford)*

A section of a panoramic photograph of the High School staff and girls in 1949. Miss Ambrose occupies the central position in the throne-like chair and is flanked by her staff. *(Janet Parkes)*

A less formal photograph of the tennis team in the 1970s. *(Christine Marks)*

Dudley Boys' Grammar School has a history going back to Elizabethan times. It arrived on the St James's Road site in 1898/9 from King Street, and was subsequently extended in 1909 and 1926. The expansion of the school was the result of the work of Hugh Watson, headmaster from 1903 until 1930. A boarding house named 'Lingwood' was opened in 1932 and another extension to the school was opened by the Bishop of Liverpool in 1936. *(NW)*

First year pupils at Dudley Grammar School, 1938/9. Two boys are wearing their Prep School blazers, indicating that they have already been at the school for a year. They are joined by a variety of fee-paying and 'County Scholarship' boys. Short trousers were generally worn until entering the second year. *(Stuart Eaton)*

Behind the windows seen here we now find the old school hall has become the library (seen below). Computers and new partitions are part of the modern school, but the library also houses many artefacts from both the Boys' and Girls' Grammar Schools.

Dudley Grammar School came under local authority control in 1945 as a result of the Education Act of the previous year. The headmaster, Dave Temple, steered the school successfully through the changes that followed this trauma and remained in post until 1962. After his departure the school had to make further adjustments, owing to the reorganisation of local government and new ideas about secondary education. Throughout these changes the school facilities expanded and were modernised, marked by various openings and ceremonies. For example, it celebrated its 400th birthday on 18 January 1962 with the Minister of Education, Edward Boyle, coming along to open new extensions. The Girls' and Boys' Grammar Schools amalgamated in 1975, and the merger with the Bluecoat School in 1989 created a comprehensive school to be known as Castle High School. Further extensions brought the Archbishop of Canterbury (George Carey) along on 20 October 1995 for their opening.

Above and below: Dudley Boys' Grammar School sports teams of 1970. Above is the cricket team with Mr West, a maths teacher. Below we see the football squads. *(Martin Pell Collection)*

Dudley Intermediate School Boxing Team of 1951, with sports master, Tom Palmer, who was also wicket keeper for Dudley Cricket Club. *(John Hingley)*

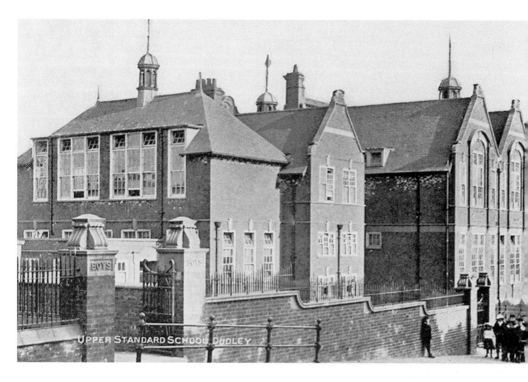

The Dudley Upper Standard School opened in 1904 in Blowers Green Road, as seen in this postcard view. It changed its name to Higher Elementary in 1912 in recognition of the growing number of pupils who were 'staying on' beyond the age of fourteen. It became the Intermediate School in 1929, and the Gilbert Claughton Grammar School in 1957. The school had been designed by Messrs Barncoft and Allcock and was built by Mark Round, Dudley's leading building contractor of that period (the foundation stone is shown on page 51). The school also provided evening classes for adults and a special section for the education of deaf-mutes. All this came to an end in 1990 and various parts of the campus have now been put to other use for community groups, etc, but the buildings are remote from the main residential areas of Dudley. *(Ken Rock)*

Barbara Williscroft (1915–81) was the first head girl of the Dudley Intermediate School and is seen here in the new school uniform with the DIS monogram incorporated into the hat badge *(Viv Turner)*

As the Gilbert Claughton Grammar School, the school maintained the 'grammar school' tradition by playing rugby. Here we see the U-12 Rugby XV of 1958. Standing, left to right: Messrs Gutteridge, Shakespeare, Grazier, Lunn, Fellows, Blewitt and teacher Mr Thompson. Seated: Messrs Hiscox, Jones, Danks, Ross (captain), Froggatt, Pearson, and Twymberrow. Front: Messrs Weyman and Bywater. *(R. Shakespeare)*

Maintaining another grammar school tradition, the Gilbert Claughton School operated a prefect system. Here we meet the prefects and upper sixth form of 1963/4. Back row, left to right: John Davies, David Smith, -?-. Middle row: Stuart Millard, William Jones, Kenneth Grazier, Roger Guest, Reginald Talbot, Gerald Winfield, -?-. Front row: Felicity Scriven, Gwynneth Hollyhead, Suzanne Parker, Victoria Price, Mr Hackett, Roger Shakespeare, Lynda Hughes, Wendy ? and Ann Saban. *(R. Hood)*

The Park Schools, taking their name from Grange Park, were fairly hidden from view. The Girls' Secondary School can just be glimpsed in this 1960s view looking up Alexandra Street. The buildings in the 'V' of Alexandra Street and Edward Street have now disappeared as completely as the schools. *(Mick Hanson via John Wythes)*

Ron Nash with the Park Secondary School for Boys football team of 1951/2. Back row, left to right: Terry Adams, Colin Round, John Wythes, ? Howells, Tony Elsley, Malcolm Fellows. Front row: Mickey Jones, Brian Large, Peter Grosvenor, Barry Whitmore and Barry Worton. Some of these boys had played against Duncan Edwards when he played for Priory School and then Wolverhampton Street, but then played alongside him in the Dudley Boys team. *(John Wythes)*

The Rosland Secondary School opened in Beechwood Road on 19 October 1932 and has this fine Dudley coat of arms over the main entrance. It was built to serve the large number of families moving into municipal housing that was constructed in the Rosland and Watson Green area. It was eventually merged with the Bluecoat School in 1970 and took the latter's name. This enlarged the intake to include pupils from the other side of Kates Hill. As the Bluecoat School, it merged with the town's Grammar Schools in 1989 to be part of Castle High School, and the buildings have been put to community use. *(NW)*

This room, just off the main hall at Rosland Secondary School, was photographed to show its conversion into the school's Adventure Club. It opened in 1968 as youth club-type facility in which pupils might return to the school in the evening to undertake training for the Duke of Edinburgh Award and socialise. It was the brainchild of headmaster Stan Hill, and the club was successfully organised by Mr W. Jones. It had an official opening by the Wolves defender, Bobby Thomson. Everything was made by the pupils themselves in woodworking and metalworking classes. *(Stan Hill)*

All that survives today of the old Wolverhampton Street schools is the caretaker's house, adjacent to a car park that was once the site of the schools. The schools were opened by the School Board in 1880 and after the Second World War became secondary modern schools which lasted until 1965 when the pupils transferred to the new Wren's Nest School. *(NW)*

The Dudley Bluecoat School opened on 19 March 1706 in Steppingstone Lane, for fifty boys. It moved to Fisher Street in 1802 where it joined forces with the Female School of Industry and then to these premises in Bean Road, Dixons Green, in the 1860s. It became a Church of England boys' elementary school in 1902 and after the 1944 Act it became a mixed secondary modern school. It moved to the Rosland School site in 1970 and survived to become one of the constituents of Castle High School in 1989 – but by then these buildings had been demolished. *(A. Warner Collection)*

Senior pupils at the Bluecoat School in about 1947. Mr Wright can be identified on the left and the teacher in the middle of the front row is thought to be Mr Garrett, but the lady on the right has not yet been identified. *(R. Hood)*

In the 1950s the headteacher was Mr A. Delacour, seen here in his gown surrounded by his staff. Next to him is Mr Wright, one of the longest-serving teachers at the school. In 1956 Mr Delacour was able to lead the school in celebrating its 250th Anniversary – commemorated at a service at Top Church. (*A. Warner Collection*)

Mr Wright appears again – on the right – in this picture of the 1950/1 Bluecoat School football team. Back row, left to right: Mr Richards, John Dyke, Ron Durrant, Denis Davies, Graham Millard, William Anslow, Mr Wright, John Fisher. Seated: Ivan Davies, Ron Spittle, John Bailey, David Probert and Ed Whitehouse. (*A. Warner Collection*)

The annual Founders' Day Procession from the Bluecoat School makes its way up Dudley High Street to Top Church in about 1960, passing the entrance to the old Temperance Institute on the left. *(A. Warner Collection)*

As a successful secondary modern the Bluecoat School eventually encouraged pupils to stay on in the fifth year to take the National Certificate of Secondary Education. The school had to equip itself with labs, craft workshops, etc., and supported a drama club and brass band, and later adopted the Duke of Edinburgh Award Scheme.

A picture of Hillcrest School, in Simms Lane, Netherton, is included here rather than the chapter on Netherton because it played a key role in establishing a prototype secondary modern school that Dudley Education Department would then seek to replicate in other parts of the borough. Hillcrest was designed by the Borough Architect, John Lewis, and built by J. Hickman of Brierley Hill. It was opened on 10 January 1958. Similar schools were later built at Holly Hall (see below), Mons Hill (1965) and Saltwells (1962). *(NW)*

Holly Hall Secondary School opened in 1966, and like Hillcrest, has survived several reorganisations in the local educational system.

These two photographs of Holly Hall Secondary School from the 1968 Borough Guide reflect the local pride felt in the new secondary schools and their modern facilities. They had at last vanquished some of the old school buildings inherited from the days of the School Board. Holly Hall later had to deal with reorganisation on 'comprehensive' lines, then became grant-maintained, and is now a foundation school calling itself the Holly Hall Mathematics & Computing College.

The library and the domestic science flat (seen above) were all seen as facilities of which Holly Hall Secondary School could be proud.

The Wren's Nest Secondary School was officially opened on 15 October 1965 and later went through a name change to the Mons Hill School after a 1974 borough-wide commitment to comprehensive education. The building, as seen here, has become the Mons Hill Campus of the Dudley Technical College, now simply calling itself Dudley College. *(NW)*

On 15 October 1965 the Wren's Nest Secondary School was opened by Viscount Cobham in his capacity as Lord Lieutenant of Worcestershire, watched by the Mayor of Dudley.

...ition in playing the guitar was available at the Wren's Nest School. Having become the Mons Hill ...econdary School in 1975, its fortunes seemed to decline and as result of falling numbers it was scheduled ...r closure in 1991. It did not quite manage to last that long as it closed in July 1990 and pupils transferred ... Castle High School, or the Coseley School. *(R. Hood)*

...he Bishop Milner Roman Catholic Secondary School opened in January 1960, with an official opening on ...1 September of that year. It was designed by the Borough Architect along the same lines as Hillcrest School ... Netherton, and has recently been considerably rebuilt. This picture is from a 1961 panoramic view of the ...chool and its pupils. The headmaster, seen slightly left of centre, was Mr Newton. *(Frank Dyce)*

Park Primary School, Nelson Street. Here we see the school's choir in 1953. Back row, left to right: -?-, Clive Mason, -?-, Arthur ?, David Loat, Roy Connop, Bernard Downing, Roger Goodridge, -?-, -?-, David Hiscox. Second row: Hazel Griffin, Margaret Garden, -?-, Jean Round, Brenda Bennett, Doreen Teague, Janet Jeavons, Dorothy Simcox, -?-, -?-, Jackie Knowles. Third row: -?-, Gillian Owens, Sandra Powell, Marilyn Wilkes, Pamela Williams, Pauline Fleetwood, -?-, -?-, -?-, Janet Dutton, Margaret Hibbert, Francis Loat. Front row: -?-, -?-, Megan Avey, Vivienne Greaves, -?-, -?-, Trevor Slimm, -?-, Mary Dudley, Janice Christopher, Valerie Hadley. *(Val Wyatt)*

Miss O'Hagan's class at St Joseph's Mixed School, 1948. This Roman Catholic school provided schooling from five to fourteen, in three stages. The 'senior' stage was replaced with the opening of the new Bishop Milner School. *(Eileen Guest)*

A wartime view looking across the Jesson's Primary School playground during a snowball fight, towards the boundary wall that followed the top of Grange Road. We can glimpse the maltings that once stood on the corner of Grange Road and Park Road, and the house that still stands at the top of Grange Road today. The schools in the Eve Hill area require a degree of explaining. St James's Primary School had been built in 1842 as a National School – i.e. a school provided by the Church of England. From 1906 onwards the school catered only for infants. Meanwhile, the Jesson's School at the top of Wolverhampton Street, on the Grange Road corner, had been established as a charity school for boys in 1856 which originally used premises at Shavers End. After the creation of the Dudley School Board the Park Schools were built in 1895 – one block containing the Boys' School, and another for Girls and Infants. The former became secondary schools after the war, and the old infants school became Park Primary School. The Park Schools closed in 1975, were demolished in 1977, and part of the site was used to build a new Jesson's School. As if all this was not complicated enough, Jesson's School had ceased to have charitable status back in 1902, and had become a Mixed School in 1927. After the closure of St James's School in 1979, the Jesson's School became a C of E School in new premises dating from 1980!

St James's School building survives, having found a new home in the Black Country Living Museum. *(NW)*

A small Cub pack was started at Park Primary School at the end of the Second World War. Back row, left to right: Laurie Hancox, John Westwood, Robert Naylor, Alan Newman. Front row: Clive Thompson, John Wythes, Roy Dyke, and Roger Leese. *(John Wythes)*

The Park Primary School football team, 1947/8. Back row, left to right: Tony Willetts, Frank Thomas, Roy Dyke, Tony Pyms (goalkeeper), John Westwood, Teddy Thomas, Joey Wilkes. Front row: Graham Woodall, Malcolm Fellows, Ray Stokes, John Wythes (captain), Lewis Marsh, Brian Elwell, and Alan Griffin. *(John Wythes)*

Catholic Schools have long been part of the education provision in Dudley. Tonia Love (seen above) was the May Queen of 1953 at St Joseph's School in Bourne Street, close to the Catholic Church. The teacher is Sister Lucy. The school has relocated to Hillcrest Road, Dixons Green. *(Irene Dyce)*

Motorists struggling up Blowers Green Road probably do not pause to stare at the end wall of Blowers Green Junior School – rather eclipsed by the neighbouring Gilbert Claughton building – but it features some nice elements of 1930s design. The architects were Messrs Butler, Jackson & Edmonds, but the noteworthy feature is the wrought ironwork around the doorway: A 'torch of learning' is featured, designed by William Bloye, who also created the statue of Apollo in Dudley's Coronation Gardens. Less obvious is the fact that the school is built on a concrete raft to protect itself from subsidence. *(NW)*

In July 1955, children at Park Junior School demonstrated what they had learned in cycling proficiency classes to the Mayor and Mayoress of Dudley, William and Rose Wakeman. *(Wakeman Collection)*

The school choir from Holly Hall Secondary School, *c.* 1948. Back row, left to right: Mr Thomas, Margaret Shuker, Mildred Ogden, Jean Drummond, Amy Emery, Fay Chilton, Elaine Harper, Janice Beardsmore, Miss Mitchell. Front row: Howard Nixon, Barry Law, -?-, Brian Davies, and Donald Malin. *(Fay & John Wythes)*

Above: The schools at Holly Hall have a complicated history – seen here in the early 1980s in their final guise as an annexe of Dudley School of Art. The buildings on the left, including the caretaker's house, were built through the generosity of Mr Cochrane of the Woodside Ironworks and opened in 1861 only to be later absorbed into the jurisdiction of the Education Committee who ran it as an infants' school and mixed elementary school of voluntary status, i.e. still partly governed by the church. It seems to have been secularised in 1910 when rebuilding took place and it became the Holly Hall Council Schools – as recorded in surviving brickwork. *(Les Gregory via Val Worwood)*

Above, right: Although much of the Holly Hall School complex was demolished in 1987, this part of the brickwork survives in the part of the building (formerly the infants' school) that is still used as a day centre. *(NW)*

Right: In this picture, taken just before demolition began, we see a side view of the school, including 'temporary' wooden classrooms on the High Street side of the complex. *(Les Gregory)*

The Holly Hall Secondary School choir of 1960. At this time it was an 'all girls' choir and it was training to take part in a Dudley Music Festival, where they sang 'Jerusalem'. Back row, left to right: Barbara Smith, Avril Guest, Diane Burton, Doreen Raybould, Brenda Brackley, Vivienne Downing, Eileen Hadlington, Phylis Cowan, Christine Hale. Third row: Iris Langford, Diane While, Lorna Nailer, -?-, Margaret Beard, Jill Billingham, Janet Davies, Kathleen Nicholls, Janet Gilks. Second row: Judith Worwood, -?-, Joyce ?, -?-, Vivienne Lewis, Mr Cartwright, Mrs Locke, -?-, -?-, Mary Tylor, -?-, Mary Reed. Front row: Elaine Mantle, Frances Roberts, Carol Checksfield, Christine Holland, Kathleen Wood, Barbara Lewis, Betty Arnold, Sandra Wheatley, and Barbara Smith. Let us consider the educational journey of some of these girls: they would have started at Holly Hall Infants School, but then gone to the new Woodside Junior School, officially opened in October 1953. After taking the 11+, they would have found themselves in the Holly Hall Secondary School – the lower portion of which was using the old Holly Hall Junior School buildings. On passing to the upper forms of the secondary school they transferred to the Stourbridge Road premises of what had been called the Harts Hill Secondary School. Some of the girls then went on to 'The Tec' – see page 86. *(Marion Mantle Collection)*

All that remains of the 1910 Holly Hall Council School – used for years as the infants' school – are these buildings which survive as a day centre run by the Social Services Department. *(NW)*

St James's School in Salop Street was a church school, and has become famous as a result of being moved stone by stone to the Black Country Museum. Here we see a fancy dress party on the lawn of St James's Church vicarage in 1951, and some, but not all of the children here would have attended the church school. The vicar, the Revd Brian Edgell, is seen to the left of the back row wearing a floppy hat. *(Val Wyatt)*

St John's School, Kates Hill, was one of three church schools in Dudley designed by William Bourne – St James's is now in the Black Country Museum, St Edmund's is now a mosque and St John's has become offices. *(NW)*

Just as St James's School in Eve Hill faced rivalry from the neighbouring secular schools, St John's in Kates Hill competed with Kates Hill Council School. Here we catch a glimpse of the building as children practice folk dancing in the playground. The school suffered a serious arson attack on 24 June 1969. (Bill Goodman)

Above and left: Kates Hill pupils photographed just before and just after the Second World War.

he staff at Kates Hill Junior School, *c.* 1955. Back row, left to right: Mr Willetts, Mrs Roberts, Mr Whitehouse. ont row: Mr Doughty, Mrs Albutt, Mr Carter (headmaster), Mrs Wood, and Miss Edwards. *(Cynthia Edwards)*

he staff at Kates Hill grew in size as a result of the junior and infants schools being amalgamated. Back ow, left to right: Ian ?, Muriel Hughes (secretary), Mrs Southan (daughter of John Molyneux), Cyril Digger, r Willetts, Nina Rogers, Mr Bellfield, Joan Armstrong. Front row: Mrs Wood, Mrs Carpenter, Miss Edwards, r Wright (headmaster), Rae Thomas, Marjorie Woodhall (secretary), and Mrs Dale (wife of Alan Dale, a ell-known figure at Dudley Teacher Training College). *(Cynthia Edwards)*

Kates Hill pupils Rebecca Plant and Louise White present Mr and Mrs Willetts with a retirement gift. Ron Willetts, seen in both pictures on the previous page, had been deput head at Kates Hill, having com to the school from Holly Hall Juniors along with Sid Carter – Kates Hill's well-remembered headmaster. Ron had been a teacher for thirty-four years, having been a local lad educat at the Grammar School, and a graduate of Dudley Teacher Training College. *(Cynthia Edwards Collection)*

Alderman Rowley, the Mayor of Dudley, is seen at the old Kates Hill Primary School on 18 February 197 The 'new' Kates Hill School in Peel Street was officially opened by his successor, Alderman Morris, c Wednesday 2 May 1973. *(R. Hood)*

The building site where the new Kates Hill Primary School was going to be built, 1972. The building of the new school coincided with much demolition of the old Kates Hill and rearrangement and renaming of the roads. Thus, in the background, we can see the old Co-op grocery and butchery shops which had been George Street and which was about to become Peel Street (see *Dudley Rediscovered* p. 125). *(School Archives)*

The Kates Hill Primary 1983/4 football team with head teacher Geoff Warburton. Back row, left to right: Shabih Naqui, Abdul Khaliq, Azim Mohammed, Anthony Cartwright, Gary Moorcroft, Nadeem Choudary. Front row: Manjeet Gill, Stephen Mellor, Jabbar Mohammed, Abdul Kazim, Matthew Round. All sport their green and yellow strip. *(School Archives)*

The primary school built to serve the Priory estate has quite a complicated history, as it struggle to keep up with the development of the estate in the 1930s. The new school was built on land onc occupied by Priory Farm. While the new school was being built, a temporary school was opened i Priory Hall, the former home of Sir Gilbert Claughton, from 1 October 1930 onwards.

When the Priory School was opened by the Mayor of Dudley, Alderman James Smellie, o 19 October 1932, only the infants were able to use the site. The juniors continued to make use of th temporary school until the summer of 1938. The Priory School campus had been augmented by th provision of a pioneering nursery school which was opened by Lady Astor on 8 March 1938, and th formal opening of the new provision for juniors was not held until early 1939!

As in all Dudley schools, there have been some bewildering changes over the years. The junior moved into what had been the original 1932 infants' school and the infants moved into the 193 junior classrooms! In 1972 the infant and junior schools changed to being infant and middl schools. In September 1985 the two schools combined simply to become Priory Primary School.

The school's most famous pupil was Duncan Edwards, born in 1936 and resident in Elm Road. H started playing football while at the school and was playing for Dudley Town Boys by the time he ha transferred to the Wolverhampton Street Secondary School. He later played for the English Junio International team, and on his sixteenth birthday was signed up for Manchester United by Matt Busb He died in February 1958 as a result of the Munich air disaster. His life is commemorated in tw stained-glass windows in St Francis's Church (see page 103).

Mr Holmes with the 1959/60 Priory Junior School football team, winners of the Collins Cup. Back row, le to right: D. Waldron, J. Winslow, K. Haden, P. Nicklin, E. Jones, P. Cole. Front row: D. Garner, J. Bradford P. Haywood (captain), R. Bradley and R. Isaac.

The Wren's Nest Junior School opened on 14 October 1936 in Marigold Crescent, but the original buildings have been replaced as part of the modernisation and regeneration of the estate. It also expanded in 2006 when the school at Sycamore Green was closed. The new buildings seen here were officially opened on 11 June 2010. Margaret Lenton and chairman of the school governors Colin Lacey led the procession in this horse-drawn carriage in front of a huge carnival parade. Margaret worked for twenty-four years at the school as cleaner, lunchtime supervisor and adult tutor in the art of flower arranging. *(NW)*

The opening of the new school building was watched by June Fownes, who has lived opposite the school for most of her life and who joined the school as a pupil in 1946. Unfortunately June was absent when her classmates were photographed in about 1950 with their teacher, Miss Morris, on the right. In the past, teachers and even caretakers became well-known Wren's Nest characters by giving long service to the school.

The Dudley & Staffordshire Technical College was opened on 13 March 1936. It absorbed the former School of Arts & Crafts in 1947, and became known simply as Dudley Technical College in 1967 – known to everyone as 'The Tec'. *(NW)*

Girls from a secretarial course at Dudley & Staffordshire Technical College on a trip to Josiah Wedgwood's premises in June 1961. The group includes Pam Marsh, Valda Maddocks, Jennifer Bowen, Marlene Henley, Vicky Yardsley, Maureen Bloor, Margaret Jefferson, Pat Hingley, Irene Shepherd, Ann Calvert, Christine Shore, Sheila Johnson, Jill Billingham, Elaine Worrall, Elaine Mantle, Barbara Lentz, Lynda Poole, Doreen Raybould, Mary Douglas and Jocelyn Naylor. Some of the others present cannot be identified. *(Elaine Mantle Collection)*

5

ESTATES

The widespread existence of poor housing was seen as one of the legacies of the nineteenth-century expansion of Dudley that had to be resolved in the twentieth century. Dudley Council did not seem to recognise that providing municipal housing would have to be a major part of the solution to the problem until after the First World War. Having decided to build 'homes fit for heroes', Dudley Council found it was short of locations where this could be delivered. An area between Kates Hill and Birmingham Road, and stretching out towards Buns Lane, provided one area, plus some other small locations, but the problem was not really solved until the council boldly purchased land outside the borough belonging to the Earl of Dudley – the Priory Estate.

The building of the Priory Estate, then the Wren's Nest and North Priory Estates is an epic tale starting in 1929 and reaching completion in the 1950s. Post-war developments like Sledmere and Yew Tree (Netherton) are often overshadowed by the spectacular growth of the Russell's Hall Estate.

The houses in Alexandra Place were built in about 1905 as workers' cottages on the Earl of Dudley's Priory Estate. They became the property of Dudley Council when the authority bought this land from the earl in 1926, and still look very attractive today. Between these houses and Bluebell Road, the council laid out Bluebell Park for the benefit of estate dwellers. The remains of a shallow paddling pool – once a feature of this park – are still in existence today. Right behind Bluebell Park, and Bluebell Road, is the Wren's Nest itself. *(NW)*

The Priory lands of the Earl of Dudley, lying in the Urban District of Sedgley, were very rural, as seen in this view across the meadow toward Castle Hill and one of its boundary lodges. This land was acquired by Dudley Corporation in 1926.

COUNTY BOROUGH OF DUDLEY
THE PRIORY ESTATE
THIS STONE WAS LAID BY
HIS WORSHIP THE MAYOR
ALD.F.J.BALLARD
ON THE OCCASION OF THE COMMENCEMENT OF
THE DEVELOPMENT OF THE PRIORY ESTATE
TUESDAY 16TH JULY 1929

After acquiring the land between Castle Hill and the Wren's Nest, Dudley Corporation had to seek legal powers to enlarge the borough's boundaries and had to begin planning the housing it wanted to build there. Private housing was to be built in Gervase Drive, Paganel Drive and Somery Drive, close to the greenery and open space provided by a new Priory Park. Priory Road was designed to be the backbone of the new estate, paralleled by Maple Road and Chestnut Road, with roads at right angles to them. Work on the municipal housing of the Priory Estate commenced on 16 July 1929, as Alderman Ballard, Mayor of Dudley, hoisted this stone into position. The stone became part of the front wall of no. 9 Oak Road (see page 91) and still survives in that position today. (Author's Collection)

Pat Collins' fairground loads, behind a Scammel 'Showtrac' tractor, pause outside the Wren's Nest public house on Priory Road in 1962. This large Mitchells & Butlers 1930s public house was renamed the Duncan Edwards from 2000 to 2006 but has since been demolished. The 'Showtrac' has been preserved. *(Roger Mills)*

Shops were part of the masterplan to which the Priory Estate was built, and occupied strategic corner locations. This shop on the corner of Oak Road and Priory Road was once a butcher's shop. It then became freezer centre and since the 1980s has been an off licence. The hairdresser's upstairs survives as a beauty salon. *(NW)*

To provide a transport link between the Priory Estate and the centre of Dudley, the Midland Red was persuaded to provide some services. The D1 ran to Forest Road, and the D2 ran to Gorse Road (on the Wren's Nest estate) via The Broadway, Priory Road, Limes Road and Laurel Road. In post-war years the D11, seen here, terminated at Mayfield Road, and the Wren's Nest can be seen in the background. *(Alan Broughall via Ron Thomas)*

Hop-pickers from the Priory Estate wait by the shops in Priory Road for a lift to the hop fields in the autumn of 1950. Some of these hop-pickers would have regularly undertaken this work before moving out to the estate. *(Tremaine Herbert Collection)*

No. 9 Oak Road – the house that was among the first to be built in the Priory Estate, seen here in 2009. Next door, at no. 11, is another plaque recording that fact that no. 11 was the home of Mr John Price who, in September 1946, became Mayor of Dudley. The first residents began moving into the estate in 1930 while it was still under construction. Most roads on the Priory took on the names of trees – while those on the Wren's Nest use the names of flowers. Houses were built as semis and foursomes and most were rendered with pebble dash which soon discoloured as a result of air pollution. New trees were planted and now provide mature tree-lined vistas to the estate's roads.

Below: Thornhill Road in April 2009 – awaiting demolition as part of the complete rebuilding of the North Priory houses. The North Priory comprised 260 houses built north of the Priory Estate at the end of the 1930s. *(NW)*

Isaac Hiscox, his wife and daughters stand outside 111 Wren's Nest Road. They are joined in the front row by Joan and Bessie Cole who lived at no. 119. The houses have been modernised and refurbished, but in 2010 no. 40 still has its original porch – similar to the one seen here! *(Elsie Garner)*

St Christopher's Church on the corner of Wren's Nest Road and Summer Road began as a mission church promoted by St Francis's in the Priory Estate. Meetings were first held in 1937 in Wren's Nest school. The foundation stone of this building was laid on 9 November 1938 and it was dedicated as a new church on 22 April 1939. By the 1970s it was abandoned as a place of worship and the church authorities decided to renovate the building with a view to it becoming a community centre. It was opened by Bobby Charlton in this new role on 18 September 1982. *(NW)*

Children make their way across Wren's Nest Road in the heart of the estate in the 1970s. Summer Road is in the background with the main shops of the estate on the left and St Christopher's Church, now the Community Centre, on the right. *(Express & Star)*

Two large 'road house'-style pubs were provided for the Wren's Nest Estate – just as the Wren's Nest pub was provided for the Priory Estate. Here we see the Washington Arms prepared for its opening on 10 December 1937. The arms shown on the inn sign carry the three stars and two stripes of the 'loyal' branch of the Washington family. The pub has now been demolished but the second estate pub, built in the 1960s, the Caves, still stands. *(Les Bywater)*

Construction of the Russell's Hall Estate began in 1957. The vast site had once been the Oak Park Colliery, which consisted of a number of small pits sprawling across this area. Mining had left a legacy of problems, among them subterranean spontaneous combustion and the possibility of subsidence. The houses, therefore, had to be built on concrete rafts. *(Alan George)*

Frank Wells outside his home at 70 Langstone Road on the Russell's Hall Estate in August 2008. These were among the first houses to be built on the estate and were completed in 1958, a year after work on the estate had begun. In 1963 Dudley opened its 10,000th council house on the Russell's Hall Estate, but the estate also included some private housing and sheltered housing. A retirement village is now to be added to the estate. *(NW)*

The houses on the Russell's Hall Estate had to be built on concrete rafts to prevent damage as a result of any subsidence and many were built in a semi-prefabricated way for lightness and speed of erection. Here, in February 1967, we see a crane unloading pre-fabricated components that had been made in Manchester, as some girls pass by on their way to Holly Hall School. *(Express & Star)*

Small details of the design of the first 400 homes built on Russell's Hall were varied to provide some individuality to the houses – for example the shape of the porch was altered. This picture was taken in May 1959, a year after the first house had been completed. *(Express & Star)*

Looking back towards central Dudley along the length of Ashenhurst Road in the 1970s. Holly Hall Scho
can be seen to the right. In the foreground is Bushey Fields Road, now leading to the hospital of the sa
name and rather hidden away behind the better-known Russell's Hall Hospital, which had not been start
when this picture was taken. The estate included shopping facilities (such as a circular branch of the Co-o
two pubs, and a church. *(NW)*

The Revd John Foottit, the curate at 'Top Church', helped gather a congregation on the Russell's Hall Esta
by organising house meetings, etc., until the construction of a church for the estate could begin. Mrs Nor
Hanson of the Dudley brewing family is seen here laying the foundation stone of St Barnabas' Church
Middle Park Road with the Bishop of Worcester on 11 June 1965 – coincidentally the saint's day. Original
it had been planned to build a church at the top of Russell's Hall Road, but this location was more centr
and the ground more stable. *(Church Archives)*

Six months later, on 4 December 1965, the Bishop of Worcester returned to the estate to open St Barnabas' Church, and the Revd John Foottit became the first vicar. The church was designed by Jennings, Homer and Lynch of Brierley Hill, and was built by S. Windsor in the functional style of the time. *(NW)*

The Revd John Foottit was vicar at St Barnabas' from its opening until 1973, and is seen here at a sale of work. At first the church was a very busy place but it has become increasingly difficult to persuade residents to make use of its facilities – even on an estate which has few others. Today the church still has a Women's Fellowship and a small Sunday School. *(Church Archives)*

As if to underline the feeling that Black Country culture is alive and well in the town's new estates, the ladies at St Barnabas' Church put on a Black Country Night Out in November 1986. Left to right: Pam Masefield, Irene Cartwright, Eileen Guest, Barbara Cole, Doris Haden and six-year-old Natalie Cooper. *(Eileen Guest Collection)*

In the 1970s St Barnabas' Church was able to preserve well-established Black Country traditions like the Sunday School Anniversary Parade in the modern surroundings of the Russell's Hall Estate. The church's banner and the St John Ambulance Brigade band helped create the right appearance of such a parade. *(Eileen Guest)*

6

CHURCHES
& CHAPELS

The centre of Dudley is often defined by the area that the town occupies between the churches of St Edmund's and St Thomas's – 'Bottom Church' and 'Top Church' – and they both rightly have an important role in the story of Dudley's development. However, the other parish churches of Dudley reflect the way that town expanded in the nineteenth century and the way that Dudley contains many districts that have a life of their own. Netherton, Eve Hill, Kates Hill, Holly Hall (Woodside), and even The Dock acquired nineteenth-century parish churches of their own. In the twentieth century the Church of England built churches in the new estates: the Priory, Wren's Nest and Russell's Hall.

This chapter also features the Non-conformists and Roman Catholics in Dudley but space does not permit us to look at the places of worship used by other faiths. Some local churches have closed and disappeared while temples and mosques have arrived on the scene.

No book on Dudley can ignore 'Top Church' as it occupies such a high-profile position in the local landscape. St Edmund's at the opposite end of central Dudley is rather overshadowed by Castle Hill, but St Thomas's and St Luke's Church – as Top Church is now correctly known – can be seen from afar. The church became the parish church of Dudley in 1646 after St Edmund's had been damaged during the Civil War. Construction of the present building began in 1816, and it was opened two years later. It can be a difficult church to photograph, but in this case the photographer has provided a rear view from part of the churchyard which was cleared to make way for the 1929 vicarage.
(*Tanfield's 'Views of Dudley'*)

The interior of 'Top Church' does not immediately reveal the extent to which it was an innovative building in its time. It is an iron-framed building and these pillars are iron, not stone. Further nineteenth-century Anglican churches were built in Eve Hill (St James'), Kates Hill (St John's), Netherton (St Andrew's), Holly Hall (St Augustine's) and The Dock (St Luke's). *(Tanfield's 'Views of Dudley')*

Tanfield's 'Views of Dudley' included one photograph of a Non-conformist chapel: the Wesley Methodist Chapel in Wolverhampton Street, built in 1829. The Baptists, Congregationalists, Unitarians, and all branches of Methodism have been well represented in the town. In 1966 this chapel became the Central Methodist Church and five local congregations merged to make current use of the building's successor.

St Francis' Church has an interesting history interwoven with the story of the development of the Priory Estate which it was built to serve. The Revd Francis Loxton was appointed to establish the church and conducted the first service on 4 October 1931 in a room in Priory Hall that was being used during the week as an infants' school. The foundation stone of the church was laid on 18 November 1931 and the building was dedicated on 6 April 1932. It was a dual-purpose building – partly serving as a church hall and partly as a temporary church until another could be built nearby. To the right is a new parish centre which was added in 1998. *(NW)*

St Francis' Church was eventually consecrated on 4 October 1949 (St Francis' Day) once it was clear that the proposed church on the corner of Limes Road and Laurel Road was not going to be built. This picture was taken a year later after the Revd David Llewellyn had become vicar and had been joined by Sister Bowmaker of the Church Army. Next to her is Stan Nock, who later wrote a good history of the church. *(Cristobel Groves Collection)*

The vicarage for St Francis' Church was another distinctive 1930s addition to the Priory Estate, but it is no longer used for that purpose. It was completed in May 1937 and the Revd Valence Powell moved in after his wedding in June 1937. Meanwhile, in 1935 another hall had been provided at the back of the church – known as the Loxton Memorial Hall. *(NW)*

Outside St Francis' Church in about 1980. Seated left to right: Gerald Wildblood, Fred Barrett, Stan Nock, Catherine Thomas, Jenny Thomas, the Revd Theo Thomas (vicar), Keith Blockley (Church Army), his mother Mrs Blockley, Tom Greenaway, Beattie Jacques, Shirley Round and Marjorie Nock. *(Cristobel Groves Collection)*

he Duncan Edwards Window at St Francis' Church
s unveiled by Matt Busby of Manchester United
27 August 1961. They were designed by Francis
eat and were funded by Manchester United,
entford Football Club, Crystal Palace Football Club
d the Wren's Nest Bowling Club, all of whom are
presented in the glasswork. There are also images
St Francis and St George. Duncan had lived at 31
n Road on the Priory Estate and attended Priory
imary School and then Wolverhampton Street
condary School. His football skills were recognised
rly on and his name will always be associated
th Manchester United as one of the 'Busby Babes'.
died as a result of the plane crash at Munich in
bruary 1958 and his funeral took place at
Francis' Church on 26 February 1958.

John's Church, Kates Hill, photographed after its
osure in 2004. *(NW)*

After the closure of St John's Church, Kates Hill, the congregation moved across the road into the Church Hall, a building designed by Messrs Webb & Gray and opened in 1932. The arrangement may have suited the congregation but the abandonment of the original church building led to the formation of a preservation group dedicated to saving St John's.

The 'Save St John's' group, led by Deb Brownlee, meet Ian Austin MP outside the church on 18 February 2009. The church was consecrated on 27 July 1840 and its construction was replicated at Eve Hill in the form of St James' Church. They were designed by William Bourne, an architect whose work is only just beginning to be valued. In a town where so much heritage has been lost, this landmark building has become a symbol of a turning point that Dudley could take if ready to adopt a new attitude to valuing its past.

The preservationists have cleared St John's churchyard revealing many interesting graves – each with a valuable local tale to tell. If the church itself can be restored, another host of details would be revealed and maintained for posterity. The twelve stained-glass windows of the church, two of which are seen here, were removed after the church's closure. Will they ever return to their original home? *(G.V. Jenkins)*

Steve Field (artist) and Astley Blake of the Vicar Street Bible Class, pose by the window made for the class to commemorate the work of Bert Bissell, founder and leader of the class. With the closure of the Vicar Street building (see next page) this window has been in need of a permanent home. *(NW)*

The Vicar Street Methodist Chapel closed on 31 August 2008, after a long history which stretched back the opening of a Primitive Methodist chapel in George Street in 1829. This was built in one of the poore and most densely populated areas of Dudley – in the vicinity of Flood Street. The congregation moved to t corner of Vicar Street and Martin Hill Street in 1902. In 1925 it became home to the Vicar Street Youn Men's Bible Class, led by Bert Bissell (1902–98). The existence of this group enabled the church to survi until 2008.

In March 1930 the *Dudley Herald* photographed queues formed outside the Town Hall, down past the library and some way beyond, to hear the evangelist Edward Jeffreys. His crusades led to the establishment of several Pentacostal fellowships in Dudley, as well as a representative of the Elim Church founded by George Jeffreys. The Brethren have ha a Gospel Hall in Hellier Street since 1931.

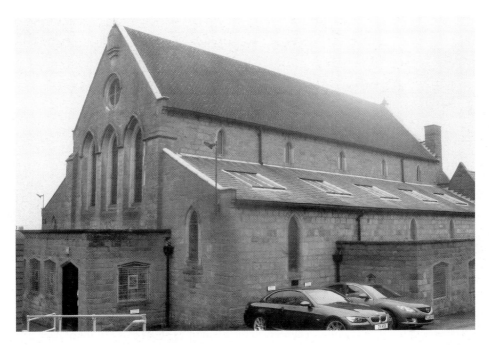

Roman Catholicism emerged from the closet after the Catholic Relief Act of 1829 and they began to build new churches in the Black Country. The Church of Our Lady and St Thomas of Canterbury was consecrated in 1842 and was designed by Augustus Pugin. This is the front of the church as seen from St Joseph Street, but most people will be more familiar with back view from Trindle Road. *(NW)*

The interior of the Church of Our Blessed Lady and St Thomas of Canterbury is spacious and very light, and much more symmetrical than Pugin's son's church at Brierley Hill. It has been a Grade II listed building since 1949. *(NW)*

The Holly Hall/Woodside area of Dudley has been served by St Augustine's Church and four Non-conformist chapels: the Wesleyans in Hall Street (now the Woodside Methodists), the New Connexion Mount Zion Chapel, High Street and the Congregationalists in High Street (both now vanished). The fourth was the Primitive Methodist chapel in The Square, now in the hands of the New Testament Church of God. It can be seen on the left in this 1960s picture as the Sunday School Anniversary Parade sets out along Holly Hall Road. *(Roy Evans)*

The New Testament Church of God congregation moved into the chapel in The Square, Woodside, in 1981, and are seen here on 30 August 2008 reopening the chapel after a major refurbishment. *(NW)*

7

NETHERTON

As explained in the introduction, Netherton is part of Dudley in local government terms, but socially it seems to have a life of its own. Had it not been incorporated into Dudley in 1865 it might well have had an independent existence as an Urban District at least until the 1930s.

It is difficult to distil the essence of Netherton into just a few pages. The presence of coalmining and of metal-bashing was stronger in Netherton than some other parts of Dudley, giving it much in common with its Black Country neighbours Brierley Hill, Quarry Bank, Cradley Heath and Old Hill but its 'public hall' survived to become an arts centre – which for a short time in the 1940s had its own repertory company. Not that Nethertonians seemed to need professional input of this sort as every chapel and church in Netherton seemed to spawn dramatic and musical talents. Ironically Netherton itself also divided into smaller local communities reminding us that the Black Country conurbation was made up of many such villages.

Heavy metal-bashing industry dominated Netherton and large chain-producing works like Noah Hingley's became complete communities in themselves where everybody lived in close proximity, worked together, drank in the same pubs and worshipped at the same chapels. Little surprise, then, that the most important day in Netherton's history seems to be 1 May 1911 when the *Titanic*'s anchor and chain left Hingley's on the first leg of its journey to Belfast. Netherton prided itself on the size of the chain that could be produced, and pictures like this are common. The chain was so heavy even the hole in the middle weighed a ton!

Two pictures of the Scouts marching through Netherton on a 1953 Coronation Parade show different aspects of the Netherton townscape. Above we see the parade passing the New Inn on the corner of Raybould's Fold, demolished in the mid-1960s, on the main (Dudley–Halesowen) road that bisects the town. This section is called High Street. Below we see that Netherton also has its leafy byways! The Scouts this time are marching up Church Road between neat inter-war three-bedroom semis, and behind the camera, huge Edwardian houses. *(Church Archives)*

Everything Dudley could do, Netherton could do! When Dudley opened a library in the 1880s, Netherton followed – and later incorporated it into a grand public hall, opened on 24 July 1894. From 1910 to 1939 the public hall itself was used to show films, and after 1947 it became the Netherton Arts Centre and home to Dudley Little Theatre. More recently it has been refurbished as the HQ of Dudley Performing Arts. Just below the public hall, in Northfield Road, was the Savoy Cinema (1936–60). It was demolished in 2004 and replaced with the Savoy Centre. Here we see a Queen Victoria lookalike emerging from the centre to open the second of Netherton's successful Victorian Fairs on 19 September 2009. *(NW)*

Two of the most famous features of Netherton are the Old Swan Inn (known to everyone as Ma Pardoe's) on the Halesowen Road – seen above in about 1910 – and the Netherton Canal Tunnel. A new link to the Birmingham Canal Navigations from the Dudley No. 2 Canal, which had almost turned Netherton into an island, was created in 1858 by the building of the Netherton Tunnel. Therefore on 20 August 2008 the 150th anniversary of the tunnel was celebrated in fine style. Cllrs Pat Martin (Deputy Mayor of Dudley) and Bob Price (Mayor of Sandwell), join Alan Smith on the stern of *The President* as part of the celebrations. *(NW)*

The history of Netherton's political clubs is told in *Netherton People & Places*. Here we see the Liberal Club on an outing in the 1930s. In the centre is Joe Darby, a founder and chairman of the club, and next to him is Sammy Dunn who ran a grocery store at the top of St John's Street. *(John Hingley)*

The Netherton Liberal Club supported several sports teams. Here we see the Liberal Club's football team of 1950, which soon afterwards became known as Parkdale Rovers. They pose for the camera with Sweet Turf Baptist Chapel in the background. Second from right in the front row is Derek Hill, who later became chairman of the Liberal Club. The goalie, in the centre of the back row, is Dennis Burchell from a well-known Cinder Bank family. *(John Hingley)*

Parkdale Rovers 1st XI in 1952/3 on the no. 2 pitch in Netherton Park. Back row, left to right: A. Willetts, A. Clift, R. Barnett, J. Smith, A. Parsons, C. Southall. Front row: J. Hingley, R. Corbett, W. Foley, R. Baker and L. Washington. *(John Hingley)*

Parkdale Rovers played in the Dudley Metro League and are seen here winning the Corbett Hospital Cup in 1976. The club lasted until 2008. *(Martin Pell Collection)*

To understand how Netherton could exist as a community quite separate from Dudley, it is worth looking at the churches and chapels of the district. Allegiance to a particular church or chapel was often a family matter and as a result of that each one had its own 'separateness' or self-contained world in which individuals grew up together, married each other and perpetuated their own closed social networks. Interaction with other such networks arose out of competition between choirs, drama groups, etc., as well as joint parades and festivals. Let's look at the process of growing up in one such chapel – St John's Methodist Chapel in St John's Street. The chapel and Sunday School building at the rear are revealed here in 2008 when the buildings in the foreground had been demolished. The congregation, originally Methodists of the New Connexion, began life in 1827 but built this chapel in 1848, followed by the Sunday School some years later. The chapel's frontage was renewed in 1898, and there were many other improvements and changes over the years. The Methodists left the building at the end of 1990 and joined the congregation in Church Road (Trinity). It has since been used by a Pentecostal fellowship. *(NW)*

When St John's closed in 1990, the sign board was photographed for posterity. It reveals that the caretaker was Fred Homer, whom we meet again on page 124. The church had started life as part of a Dudley circuit and then became part of Cradley Heath circuit. *(Barbara Gwinnell)*

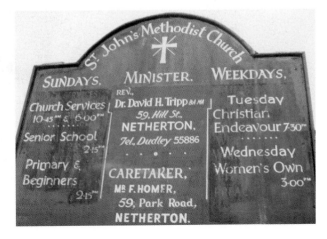

The organ at St John's Chapel was installed in 1882 and underwent thorough refurbishment in 1950 and 1977. When the chapel closed at the end of 1990, the organ was given to a church in Madagascar and is presumably still there. Colin Detheridge, who appears as choirboy (front left) in the picture on the next page, was the chapel's last organist. (*Barbara Gwinnell*)

The present generation of ex-St John's Methodists, now absorbed into the congregation of Trinity Methodist Church in Church Road, can look back on the traditional way in which their lives had progressed socially via their church. Here we see them joining the Junior Christian Endeavour Group which met on Tuesday nights, led by Clarrie Siviter . . . not to be confused with the Youth Group which met on Fridays. Christian Endeavour met for devotional purposes and sang hymns accompanied by Mrs Jackson on the harmonium. The emphasis was on the idea of 'service to others' and the various groups competed with each other to win the Junior Challenge Banner seen in the background of this mid-1950s picture. (*Barbara Gwinnell*)

Children could graduate from Christian Endeavour to the Junior Choir, started and trained by Bill Detheridge, who is seen on the left. The choir competed in a local inter-chapel eisteddfod held at the Arts Centre. In the centre of the picture is Isaiah Owen, the Sunday School Superintendent. *(Barbara Gwinnell)*

Chapel-goers could also join the St John's Amateur Operatic Society, seen here in the production of *San Marino* presented in March 1952. The show was produced by Ben Guest with musical direction by Jack Hadley and a cast that reads like a 'Who's Who' of St John's, including Bill Detheridge, William Plant, Gerald Crewe, Doris Smith and Millie Wakeman. Children from the Sunday School also participated in the Netherton Music & Drama Festival – not to be confused with the chapel's own eisteddfod. *(Barbara Gwinnell)*

Music accompanying the shows at St John's Chapel was provided by Jack Hadley's Orchestra. Jack, who played the piano, is seen in the centre of the front row in this picture and his band included Messrs Howe and Randal on first violins, Messrs Garland and Tilley on second violins, Mr Wainwright on cello and Mr Cartwright on the drums. Jack Hadley was a partner in the garage on Halesowen Road trading as Mason & Hadley. *(Barbara Gwinnell)*

The musical and dramatic traditions at St John's, like the other Netherton chapels, went back a long way and was perhaps at its height between the wars. Here is the cast of *The Merry Milk Maids* in about 1938. Left to right: Cissie Edmunds, Millie Wakeman, Gwen Plimmer, -?- and Cissie Brown. Amateur drama thrives today at the Netherton Arts Centre in the form of Dudley Little Theatre. *(John Hingley)*

On 27 September 1975 Sandra and Jeff Jones were married at St John's Chapel. As can be seen from the picture below, the chapel interior has changed very little despite the departure of the organ. *(Sandra Jones)*

The present congregation using the St John's Street building is an independent Pentecostal group which first met in the Kates Hill area of Dudley. When photographed in July 2004 they were led by the Revd Desmond McDonald. *(NW)*

The March 1953 production at St John's was *The Pirates of Penzance* featuring Bill Detheridge, Lawson Mansell, Bill Beard, Sidney French, Gerald Crewe and Millie Wakeman. By the 1960s the folks at St John's were producing a series of Whitehall farces. Today amateur musical shows come to the Arts Centre via the work of Quarry Bank Amateur Operatic Society. *(Barbara Gwinnell)*

Dudley Wood and Darby End had their own shows to demonstrate their independence from central Netherton! Here at Easter 2010 we find the Cole Street Methodists maintaining that tradition with their play, *Angel's Circus*, supported by a choir from not only Cole Street Chapel, but also Trinity and Dixon's Green. As in other parts of the Dudley and the Black Country, chapels in Netherton have merged following closures. *(NW)*

The churches and chapels of Netherton have a history of independence but in recent years have often worked and worshipped together. Here we see the congregations of St Peter's Church of Windmill End and Cole Street Methodists of Darby End marching together to an open-air service on the Withymoor Playing Fields in 1990. They are passing St Peter's Church, which was built as a mission church with a history going back to the 1870s. This building dates from 11 January 1913 and acquired parish church status in 1977, but is now back under the wing of St Andrew's. *(John Willetts)*

The same procession marches past the Cole Street Methodist Chapel – a building which opened on 3 October 1959, replacing a building of 1904 vintage but used by a congregation which had began life almost a century earlier. *(John Willetts)*

Chapel congregations would break away and assert their independence for a variety of reasons – sometimes retaining that independence, sometimes merging with others. The folks at the Wesley Bible Institute in Cole Street broke way from the other Wesleyans in Cole Street before the First World War. They first met in a corrugated iron building and then erected a brick building in 1915. Here we see a harvest festival service at the Wesley Bible Institute in 1947. The organ at the back of the picture has now been moved to the side of the chapel. *(John Willetts)*

Here we see Sydney Foley and Nellie Walker opening a new brick-built Sunday School extension in 1963. *(John Willetts)*

The Wesley Bible Institute owned a fine professionally made Sunday School banner, seen here with John Weaver and Sam Smith on the left and John Willetts on the right. *(John Willetts)*

The People's Mission Hall in Swan Street has also preserved its traditional Sunday School banner, seen here at a Sunday School event on 13 June 2004. Brian and Avril Payton are conducting the children from the front pew. The mission opened in a corrugated iron chapel in Swan Street in 1898, and moved into the building seen here in 1934. *(NW)*

Space was devoted in *Netherton People & Places* to the stories of the men and women who have played a part in the township's history, but such a task can never be completed. This book has chosen John Molyneux to represent the people who devoted their lives to Dudley. Here Fred Homer is chosen to represent Nethertonians. Fred Homer was born on 15 March 1919 in St Thomas's Street, and attended Brewery Street School. He became a chargehand toolsetter at Stewart & Lloyd's Coombes Wood Works, where he worked all his life. He began to take an active part in local politics in the late 1950s and served on Dudley Council for thirteen years. Here he is seen holding a framed letter from Margaret Thatcher thanking him for his work for the Conservative cause. He was also a school governor and Chairman of Netherton Allotment Society. At St John Chapel he was Primary Sunday School Superintendent from 1945 until 1990, and was caretaker from 1955 until closure in 1990. He walked everywhere – to and from work, and in pursuit of his many activities in Netherton and Woodside. He died in 1992. *(Barbara Gwinnell)*

John T. Bill was born at 71 Cradley Road, Netherton, on 17 June 1882. Like many others who lived in that part of Netherton, he went to work at Hingley's and served for fifty years as a chainmaker. He was also a member of the congregation at Primrose Hill Congregational Chapel. At that chapel, a second home to many workers at Hingley's, he married Anna Louisa Barnsley, who was also from Netherton. Here they are seen with their daughter Edith.

John T. Bill's claim to fame was based on his determination to be a poet and songwriter. He also wrote hymns. His first book of poetry was published in 1928 in the form of a little book called *Tiny Buds* which was published by A. Savage of Netherton, and sold for sixpence.

wards the end of his life John Bill lived
4 Wolverhampton Street, Dudley, and
hen he heard that the queen was going
visit Dudley on 23 April 1957 he
cided to produce a book of poems that
ould mark the occasion. The result was
anthology called *Highlights of Dudley*.
hn Bill died in 1962.

Here we see the cover of the sheet
usic for John Bill's song, 'As Long As The
noke Goes Upward' – The Chainmaker's
ng, which features a picture taken at
ngley's.

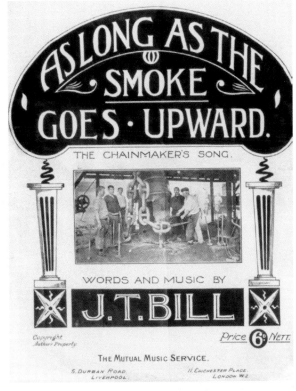

etherton's most famous resident today
Alan Smith, known to everybody as
ynuk, the surviving member of the
omedy duo, Aynuk and Ayli. Alan was
orn on 14 October 1937 in Netherton
nd is a veteran of Black Country comedy
ntertainment. John Plant, born in 1951,
as the third Ayli to appear alongside
lan's impersonation of Aynuk. Alan died
November 2006 and since that time Just
ynuk has been a solo act.

Alan developed the characters of Aynuk
nd Ayli from stories used by Dudley-born
usic hall comedian Ernie Garner. Harry
elton joined him as the first Ayli and
ey performed as part of the concert
arty at Cole Street Methodist Church in
964. Alan had worked for the Netherton
rm of F.H. Jennings and had run his
wn businesses before deciding to go
rofessional as Aynuk. He and his wife
lollie married at St John's Church, Kates
ill, in 1959 and since that time they have
ttended St Andrew's Church, Netherton,
here Alan is now a member of the PCC.

Netherton commemorates Remembrance Sunday with its own ceremony and parade. The War Memorial is in front of the parish church and here we see the wreath-laying ceremony about to begin in November 2007. *(NW)*

Netherton Church of England School football team, 1947. Back row, left to right: D. Turner, Mr Griffiths (sports master), Mr Simpson (headmaster), B. Hughes. Middle row: J. Hingley, J. Hall, R. Barnett, J. Smith, P. Nicklin, B. Owen, L. Farmer. Front row: A. Willetts, T. Postin, J. Hulme, C. Aston, K. Hall. *(John Hingley)*

therton enjoyed a pioneering place in the history of local nursery education, with the opening of childcare centre for the children of working mothers in the park during the Second World War. The rthfield Road schools also provided a nursery during the 1940s and the children at that nursery are seen re saying their prayers while sitting in a circle. Some are wearing their smocks. *(Michael Kirby)*

e children at Northfield Road's nursery wore a smock, seen very clearly in this picture of the children ting at a table. At the head of the table is Michael Kirby who came to live in Netherton with his mother d grandparents while his father was on wartime service. Michael's grandmother was Sarah Whitehouse ho ran a pawn shop at 42 High Street. His grandfather was Daniel Hancox Whitehouse who had been a beral councillor since 1935. *(Michael Kirby)*

ACKNOWLEDGEMENTS

A large number of people helped me compile the two Netherton books and the previous Dudley book and have been identified in those books. It seems more appropriate to simply add the names of the people who have been of great assistance while working on this book.

Malcolm Bagley, Bill Hampton, Sidney Evans, Tremaine Herbert, Chris Marks, Maureen Dupont, Mick Coyle, Judith Round, Alan Wycherley, John and Pam Pestana, Suzanne and Bill Hazelton, Valerie Wyatt (née Hadley), Cynthia Edwards, Eileen and Ron Guest, Horace and Elsie Garner, Frank and Irene Dyce, Jill Morgan, Michael Kirby, John Willetts, John and Fay Wythes, Barbara and Les Gwinnell, Jeff and Sandra Jones, John Hingley, Colin and Barbara Detheridge, Val Worwood, Elaine Pugh, Christobel Groves, G.V. Jenkins, and Alison and Malcolm Pell.

There is another group of people who have been thanked before but need to be thanked again for a very specific input into this book. These include: Stan Hill, Roger Crombleholme, Eric Bytheway, Trevor Brook, Ken Rock, Roger Hodson, June Sidaway, Joyce Garner, Frank Wells, Stuart Eaton, Viv Turner, Deb Brownlee, A. Warner, Alan George, Roger Mills, Bill Goodman, Elaine Mantle, Les Gregory and Val Wyatt.

I am grateful for help from the *Express & Star*, the *Black Country Bugle*, and the folks at the Bumble Hole Conservation Centre, and for assistance at the Dudley Archives & Local History Centre. Terri Baker-Mills has mopped my brow and provided encouragement throughout the proceedings.

I am happy to hear comments from readers and discuss future projects via my website: www.nedwilliams.co.uk

On a final note I'd like to reassure readers with a reminder that Netherton and parts of Dudley, as a result of being on an ex-coalfield, are prone to subsidence and might fall down. Here we see a scene in Dudley Market Place on Friday 24 August 1934 when everyone woke up to find that Peacock's Store had collapsed overnight. Fortunately nobody was killed or injured in this incident.